D0668976
Dr. Shay Roop
for Women Only
To Betty! Good luck to you for a long & sensational life.
Love, Shay

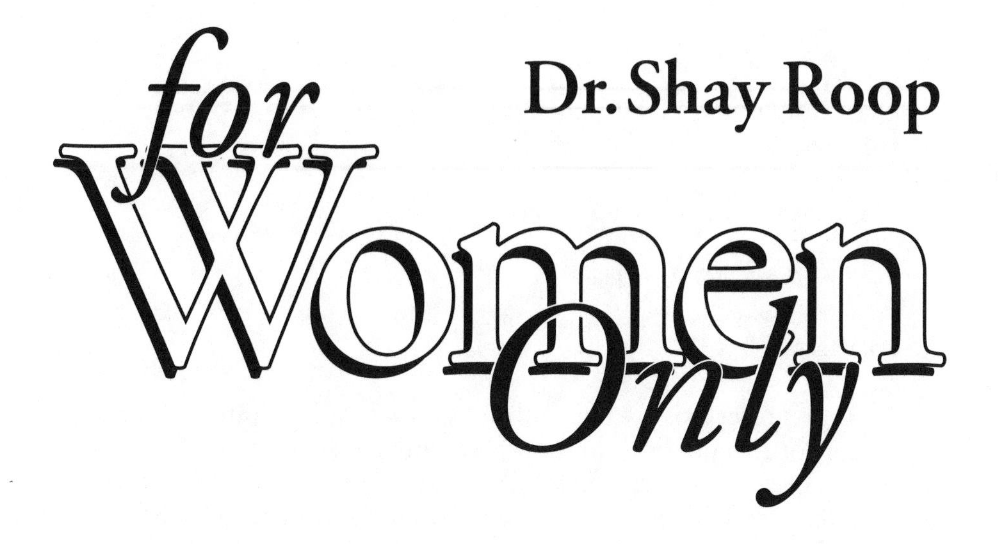

Dr. Shay Roop

God's Design for Female Sexuality & Intimacy

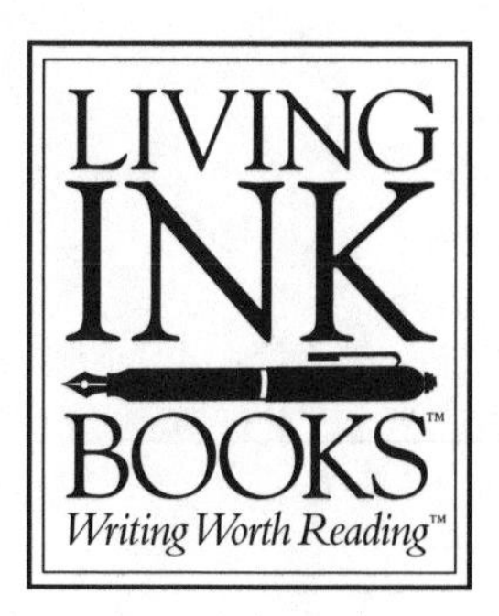

For Women Only: God's Design for Female Sexuality and Intimacy

Published by AMG Publishers
6815 Shallowford Rd.
Chattanooga, TN 37421

ISBN 0-89957-135-2

First printing—July 2004

Cover designed by Market Street Design, Chattanooga, Tennessee
Interior design and typesetting by Reider Publishing Services, West Hollywood, California
Edited and Proofread by Renée and David Sanford, Sanford Communications, Inc., Portland, Oregon; Dan Penwell, Sharon Neal, and Warren Baker

Printed in the United States of America
09 08 07 06 05 04 –V– 8 7 6 5 4 3 2 1

With love to my husband, Bob.

He invested his life in mine.

He challenged me to dare to dream and develop my passion.

He motivated me to think that all things were possible and empowered me to believe that they were.

He inspired me to believe in my own ability and God's sovereignty.

He said, "Grow old along with me, the best is yet to be"—and he was right.

CONTENTS

PART II
THE PHYSIOLOGY OF SEX

PART III
THE COMPLEXITY OF SEX

PART IV
THE ENRICHMENT OF SEX

Acknowledgments

This whole book would never have been written without the instigation and step-by-step direction of my precious friend, Judy Carden. From her teaching me how to write a book proposal to sending me to the Florida Christian Writer's Conference and introducing me to our superb literary agent, she has been a wonderful source of information and help.

Grateful thanks go to my wonderful acquisitions editor and friend, Dan Penwell, who was the first one to encourage me to write this book after seeing my proposal. He has been a constant source of encouragement and enthusiasm throughout the whole process.

Immense gratitude goes to all the people who proofread sections for me and allowed me to quote them, giving this book the scope it has: Dr. Paul Vazquez, Teresa Vazquez, Dr. Jeff Jensen, Rev. Randy Evans, Father John Hyers, Nancy Coker, Dr. Cory Hammond, pharmacist Scott Snyder, Vivie Dimmitt, Linda Miner, and my dear sister, Nancy Cunningham, who gave me my first sexual education.

I am indebted to my fantastic editors, Renée Sanford and her husband, David, who head up Sanford Communications, Inc., for all their hard work.

Much appreciation goes to my wonderful children Kelly, Steve, and Laura, as well as my "son-in-love," Patrick, for their encouraging kudos all along the way. Great thanks goes to Patrick for all his outstanding computer help.

True recognition must go to all my amazing clients who have allowed me the privilege to be privy to their most delicate secrets and sensitive issues. Though their names have been changed within these pages, they are the heroes of this book and it was my honor to serve them. They truly make every day a pleasure for me and the exciting reason I get to go to work.

Dear Reader~

My heartfelt desire is that this book will inform you of your God-given sexuality, answer some of your questions, make you laugh, and make you cry.

My hope is that, instead of thinking that you are the only woman who struggles with sexual issues, you will see that you are not alone and that you will find help and hope in these pages. You may not agree with everything I've written, but I trust that you will be challenged in your thinking by what you've read.

My aspiration is that the information will draw you closer to your husband and your husband closer to you.

My prayer is that these real life stories will enlighten you, encourage you, and assist you in understanding the gift of your sexuality so that you may have a richer life and have it more abundantly.

Shay

Introduction

Love is patient, love is kind. . . .
Love does not delight in evil but rejoices with the truth.

1 Corinthians 13:4, 7

Love your neighbor as yourself.

Mark 12:31

This book is written directly to women, for women, about women by a woman. It comes from years of counseling women regarding sexual issues and being constantly amazed at the dearth of knowledge that American women possess when it comes to this important subject.

When I grew up sex was always spelled or whispered. It was never said out loud.

"Did you hear about Cousin Lily? She was dating that Carson boy and they had S-E-X and now they are getting married."

The subject of sex was always filled with mystery, and too often, ignorance, because my "source" was the girl down the street who made up the parts she didn't know about. It wasn't until I got enough nerve to ask my sister about sex that I got some healthy information.

I learned early that the worst enemy of good sexual information is silence. Since my sister was ten years older than I was, she gave me age appropriate information and then gave me updates as I grew older. For instance, when I first found out about other positions for sex aside from the "missionary" position, I was sure these other positions were done only by prostitutes. I breathed a sigh of relief that it wouldn't be expected of me. Imagine my surprise when my sister told me prostitutes were not the only women who used other positions! I was afraid her night job was *not* at the library!

As I learned more about sexuality I had a hard time believing God could be part of this, let alone have invented it. But there it was in black and white, in verses such as 1 Corinthians 7:3, which says, "The husband should fulfill his marital duty to his wife, and likewise the wife to her husband." The more I learned about intimacy and marriage the more I realized that sex was a big part of God's plan for bonding us to our partners. He created how the two became one flesh. He never meant for sex to be *everything* in marriage, but certainly he designed it as one type of "glue" that enhances that divine amalgamation.

I have rarely talked with a couple who had a loving, sexually intimate relationship that wasn't able to work through conflicts.

Since sexuality is a form of communication, the health of a couple's intimacy is a good indicator of the health of their relationship. Conversely, when there is unresolved anger, resentment, or unmet bonding needs, it usually evidences itself in the bedroom.

That may be one reason why God tells us in Ephesians 4:25–27 to "speak truthfully . . . 'In your anger do not sin': Do not let the sun go down while you are still angry, and do not give the devil a foothold." God knows that conflicts that are not resolved will eventually erode our intimacy and drive a wedge into all other areas of our oneness.

Many Christian women suffer with problems in intimacy because they assume it is biblical to put everyone else's needs before their own. If that were always true, why would God tell us to love our neighbor as much as we love ourselves? Healthy self-love is akin to caring responsibly for our bodies, the temple of the Holy Spirit. The love described in 1 Corinthians 13 should guide and shape all of our relationships. I believe that God intends for us to be patient, kind, truthful, protecting, and persevering when it comes to ourselves, and, thus, to our God-given sexuality, as well.

Some women have let time pressures, stress, and the urgent exhaust them, leaving nothing for themselves or their sexuality. Too often I hear the cry from women that they are "too tired" for sexuality with their mates. Some thought everyone "endured" sex as they did. Many, many women have had nowhere to turn for information or education.

I believe Jesus brings abundant life (John 10:10) to all areas of our being. It's time to have it more abundantly in the realm of our sexuality. Sexuality is one area where many women—approximately 40 percent—are having major difficulties, let alone abundance.

My prayer is that this book will break all the old archaic rules of silence about educating women about their sexuality and that God will pour out his deep riches, wisdom, and knowledge. "For from him and through him and to him are all things. To him be the glory forever!" (Rom. 11:36).

PART I
The Psychology of Sex

CHAPTER 1

BONDING

I love a hand that meets my own
with a grasp that causes sensation.

SAMUEL OSGOOD

Dr. Shay, I can't seem to find the right man for me. Look at me, I'm twenty-eight and still not married. I find someone and for about two years I think he is wonderful. But then something happens, and I just lose interest. I've finally figured out the problem must lie with me. Can you help me?"

Jane had the same difficulty that many women have had. She would find the perfect man, would remain with him for a time, but then the glow would begin to fade. She believed that, as soon as those exciting feelings wore off, it wasn't love anymore. She had many questions. Did she pick men who really did change dramatically over a few years? Did she have major bonding problems? And does bonding start and stop? Well, yes and no.

Attachment bonding can be related to certain behaviors that parents exhibit in bonding with their babies. This bonding sets the stage for better adjustment all through our lives. Studies show that 85 percent of our personality is set by age six, making good attachment bonding vitally important!

Parental engrossment describes the characteristics that occur when the parents are engrossed and begin to bond with their infant. Pay special attention to these behaviors and you will see that many of these same characteristics can be seen later during the courtship phase of intimacy.

1. Absorption, preoccupation and interest, including visual awareness and focusing on the beauty of the child.
2. Tactile awareness, focusing on holding, stroking, kissing.
3. Awareness of distinct positive physical characteristics.
4. Perception of the baby as "perfect."
5. Development of a feeling of very strong attraction to the baby.
6. Experiencing a feeling of elation while with the baby.
7. Experiencing a deep sense of satisfaction and self-esteem.
8. Increased blood pressure, pulse, and respiration while interacting with the baby.

While these intensive behaviors tend to wane as the child gets older, this early attachment gives the baby security. Good attachment early in life helps enable them to "break away" during later stages of development, when curiosity and gradual individuating from the parents is healthy and beneficial.[1]

Jane was a victim of serial infatuation. In the process of therapy it became evident that Jane was immature and possibly in love with the *feelings* of infatuation, but she was not able to move into the next healthy stage of adult attachment. In 1 Corinthians 13, we read all about the characteristics of love. In this same passage we also find that, as we grow into adulthood, we put away childish understandings and concepts. We move into unselfish maturity which brings us security, reduced anxiety, calmness, and greater love in our relationships.

The men Jane chose may have been able to go on to a more mature, steady relationship—but she wanted the "high" and immediate gratification of immature infatuation. As soon as the ecstatic feelings wore off she assumed that she didn't love them anymore and moved on. When we identified and explored her past and I explained how God intended for bonding to work, she realized she may have broken up with some men who could have been very good for her.

Stages of Infatuation

Anthropologist Helen Fisher writes about infatuation in her book, *The Anatomy of Love.* I have paraphrased and condensed some of the stages of infatuation she describes.

Flirting is the first stage of the infatuation process. Females generally start the flirting process by smiling at an admirer and then looking down and to the side. The female may then cover her face with her hands and giggle nervously. Unknowingly, she may then raise her shoulders and toss her hair in a sweeping motion.

Then *staring* begins. The couple may look intently into each other's eyes for a few seconds and then look away. If the staring continues, the couple's pupils dilate, signaling interest.

After the gaze, men typically *smile* back, in time walk over to the female, arch their back and thrust out their chests—probably without even realizing it. This may be the male's way of beginning the "courting dance."

So it may not be the heart that signals the beginning of romance, says Fisher, but the eye. Perhaps this is why the Bible urges us to watch out for the "lust of the eye" (1 John 2:16).

Next in the flirting process come *talking, mild affection,* and *body synchrony.* Synchrony is when one person mirrors another. Both people swivel their bodies until their shoulders are aligned and their bodies are face-to-face. If the woman smoothes her hair, the man will also smooth his hair; when he crosses his arms, she will cross hers as well. They begin to move in perfect rhythm while they gaze at each other. Total body synchrony signals the end of the flirting process and the beginning of infatuation, when the partner takes on special meaning.

Other senses come into play. A woman may state that she likes the way he smells. Since we have millions of olfactory (sense of smell) nerves at the bases of our brains, and women perceive smells much more than men, smell becomes a big factor in romance. The olfactory nerves connect to the limbic system, which contains the seat of long-term memory, so a person can remember odors years after smelling them. Just as old songs bring back memories, so do familiar smells. My grandmother (now deceased) wore a certain face powder that, when I smell it now, I'm right back with her. Sight and hearing perceptions can fade much more quickly than smell or olfactory perceptions.

Fisher tells us that Napoleon reportedly sent a letter to his love stating, "I will be in Paris tomorrow evening. Don't wash." While Napoleon liked the odor of his unwashed lover, today many of the complaints I hear from women about their husbands is that they

Top Ten Turnoffs for Women

1. Body odor
2. Beard stubble/dirty hair
3. Bad breath
4. Grabbing at a woman's breasts or genitals
5. No connection all day, then husband wants sex at 11:00 PM
6. Rude language
7. Roughness
8. Lack of enough foreplay
9. Husband who views pornography
10. Husband who constantly wants sex

don't wash enough. Poor hygiene is one of the top ten turnoffs women list regarding lovemaking.

Whenever my husband and I counsel a couple we always mention the extra ability of females to perceive odors and explain why cleanliness is so important to most women as a prelude to sex. Men will tell us, "I get turned on by her when she's sweaty," and we have to tell them that the reverse is rarely true for women.

Some women also tell me they like to be clean themselves before intimacy and feel uncomfortable if they haven't showered. They feel as if their normal body smells are offensive to their husbands.

Almost everyone can remember the feelings of infatuation—the euphoria, the daydreaming about a special someone. While sitting in a boring high school class, I would often write my name as Mrs. Shay ________, and then insert my boyfriend's last name. I tended to long for my next date, stay by the phone hoping he'd call, be ecstatic if he did and totally dejected if he didn't. These were all signs of the beginning euphoria of infatuation. Then when I would see my boyfriend, my heart would beat faster, my palms would sweat, and I would feel giddy or silly, talking until dawn; and I would have limitless energy and become oblivious to all others.

As infatuation progresses, a woman can have continued thoughts of the loved one that almost becomes obsessive. Hoping the relationship will go somewhere, yet feeling unsure of whether it will or not, often causes us to struggle. Replaying any positive thing the other said builds the case for the former. Games like "he loves me, he loves me not" go on in the mind as the partners vacillate back and forth on the other's intentions.[2]

It almost seems as if these feelings are not under voluntary control. As we will discuss later in this chapter, God-ordained biochemistry plays a big part in the plethora of emotions, whims, and actions that accompany infatuation.

Following a Lovemap

Besides infatuation, what else dictates the reason a woman may choose John over Joe? For years, psychologists have used the old adage that we marry our mother, father, sibling or some combination of them. We tend to be attracted to the personality or physical traits of someone in our early lives. Sexologist John Money coined the phrase "lovemap" in his book *Lovemaps*. He contends that very early in life, between ages five and eight, we develop mental maps or patterns in response to family or friends or a combination thereof.[3]

This unconscious template may take shape and form because of the way your mother listened to you or rocked you, or the way your father smelled or walked or acted. Certain personality traits were positive for you, others negative for you, but the lovemap was formed from negatives and positives of these first people you fell in love with. Years before Mr. Right or Mr. Wrong walked up to you at a party, you had already developed some vital elements of your model man.

However, at times the lovemap can have mostly negative characteristics and this may be the reason some people continue to make the same poor choice for a mate two, three, or even four times. First, infatuation may blur our view of the person. Perhaps that is why we say "love is blind" and that we "wear rose-colored glasses" while in love. We pick partners with the negative characteristics in our lovemap, but we don't see them as negative until after the marriage. Again, it may not always be the heart, but the mind's eye following our lovemaps.

Of course without the awareness of where this compulsion comes from to pick these types of people, the woman simply believes that she is making better choices each time. I believe that awareness of why we do things can protect us from being in denial about the character of other people. Otherwise, we continue to choose negative and even destructive relationships.

Created for Bonding

Again, this madness of infatuation has an amazing link to our biochemistry. An area in our brain known as the limbic system governs our basic emotions—Fear, Love, Anger, Sadness, and Happiness. If you use the acronym FLASH, you can remember the first letter of each of these five basic emotions. When we experience these feelings, parts of the limbic system are producing electrical and chemical reactions.

In 1983, psychiatrist Michael Liebowitz of the New York State Psychiatric Institute suggested that the exhilaration of romantic attraction is due to a brain bath of one or more natural stimulants, among them PEA (short for phenylethylamine), dopamine, norepinephrine, and serotonin. In the right doses, dopamine and norepinephrine give one feelings of euphoria and exhilaration.[4]

It is believed that during infatuation our neurons in the limbic system become saturated or sensitized by these powerful brain chemicals and stimulate our brain. It's not hard to see why we can stay up all night talking, be so energetic, feel extra happy, and be lively. When we are infatuated, we're "high" on God's natural amphetamines, geared to bond us to each other. So in part, the feeling of infatuation may come from a dose of PEA and other chemicals that act as natural stimulants, which transform our senses and alter our perceptions of reality.[5]

Scientists suspect that brain chemistry is also responsible for the end of infatuation. Infatuation tends to last from about eighteen months to three years. Theories maintain that the brain cannot eternally create that state of bliss. Either the nerve endings become habituated to the chemicals or levels of PEA and other chemicals begin to drop.[6]

It appears that God uses certain brain chemicals to allow us to bond to someone—but how does he keep us bonded? Leibowitz, author of *The Chemistry of Love,* contends that as infatuation wanes adult attachment takes over. A new group of brain chemicals, the endorphins, or endogenous morphines, are produced. Unlike the high of PEA, the endorphins calm us, reduce anxiety, and fill us with safety. While the bonding process is exciting, adult attachment is more warm, comfortable, and secure. This stage grows deeper and richer with care and cultivation of the relationship.[7]

I'm awed by the immense detail God has incorporated to enable us to enjoy our world. He has crafted our bodies and minds with exquisite detail to help us bond and have intimacy. Psalm 8:3, 4 expresses it well:

> When I consider your heavens,
> the work of your fingers,
> the moon and the stars,
> which you have set in place,
> what is man that you are mindful of him,
> the son of man that you care for him?

We are truly fearfully and wonderfully made!

Points to Consider

1. Bonding begins with infatuation and the particular behaviors associated with it.
2. Scientists believe certain brain chemicals that are secreted during infatuation and adult attachment contribute to the bonding process.
3. Besides infatuation, lovemaps dictate how we choose a mate.
4. A lovemap is made up of characteristics from the first people we fall in love with—our early caregivers.
5. A lovemap can have characteristics which are positive, negative, or a blend of both.

CHAPTER 2

Bonding Needs and Stages

The fragrance always stays in the hand that gives the rose.

Hada Bejar

Once we have bonded with someone, we want that attachment to grow and expand. We can do this better by comprehending our bonding needs. Beginning with the creation of Adam and Eve, God designed all peoples to be in relationships. God often uses other people as his instruments to meet our needs, especially when it comes to relational bonding needs.

All of us have bonding needs, but we usually have one or two that are more crucial than the rest. As you read through the list below, you may want to choose the two that seem most important to you. Possibly, these may be needs that weren't fulfilled completely in childhood. You may want to work on meeting some of these needs for yourself or in a relationship. Ferguson and Thurmond developed this list in *The Pursuit of Intimacy.*[1]

Ten Crucial Bonding Needs

1. **Acceptance.** To experience a deliberate and ready reception with a favorable response (Rom. 15:7).
2. **Respect.** To hold in high regard or esteem (Rom 12:10).
3. **Attention.** To convey interest and thought to another (1 Cor. 12:25).
4. **Empathy/comfort.** To give consolation with tenderness (1 Thess. 4:18).
5. **Appreciation.** To communicate gratefulness with words and feeling (1 Cor. 1:4).
6. **Security.** To have confidence of harmony; freedom from harm (Mark 6:50).
7. **Support.** To come alongside and gently help carry a load (Gal. 6:2).
8. **Approval.** Expressed commendation; positive affirmation (Rom. 14:18).
9. **Affection.** To communicate care and closeness with physical touch (Rom. 16:16).
10. **Encouragement.** To urge forward and positively persuade toward a goal (Heb. 10:24).

When I counsel couples about these needs, usually their first response is to tell their partner what their top two bonding needs are and expect the partner to be 100 percent responsible for meeting those needs. We explain that the partner can meet some of the needs but each person can also help fulfill some of their own bonding needs.

Men and women should get their intimacy needs met from their spouse, from other adult family and friends, and from God. When we don't get the needs met in those three healthy places we are apt to turn to unhealthy substitutes. Men can turn to work, alcohol, drugs, pornography, or other women. Women tend to turn to food, work, addictions, or their children.

Adults were put on this earth to meet their children's needs, but women who use the children to meet their own intimacy needs are hurting their children. Children need to be allowed to grow up just being kids, not being burdened with thinking, *Mom is sad, so what can I do to make her happy?* If the children grow up trying to meet mom's needs, they don't learn how to experience their own feelings and meet their own needs.

How to Meet Your Own Bonding Needs

Most women choose attention and affirmation as their top two intimacy needs. They tend to be somewhat critical of themselves and are looking for their husbands to make them feel better about themselves. They may have inner critical, negative messages that are absolutely contrary to what God says about them. I teach them to debate those messages with truthful statements. As women, we can give ourselves affirmation and approval with positive statements by recognizing we are made in God's image and that he reigns over our entire lives.

Through the death and resurrection of Jesus Christ and our belief and trust in him, we are acceptable to God (2 Cor. 5:21). The better we are able to accept ourselves as God accepts us, the stronger and healthier our relationships and love bonds will be. I encourage women to memorize healthy self-affirming biblical statements such as:

I am loved with an everlasting love (Jer. 31:3).
I am free of shame and condemnation (Rom. 8:1).
I am strong in the Lord (Eph. 6:10).
I am beloved and chosen by God (1 Thess. 1:4).
I will not fear since God's perfect love casts out fear (1 John 4:18).

At times women have difficulty affirming themselves because of mistakes they made earlier in life. I lead them to the insight that though we may make mistakes, *we ourselves are not a mistake.* Mistakes are not proof of inadequacy—they are wonderful opportunities to learn. Self-respect comes from thinking of ourselves with the esteem God gave us when he deemed us so valuable that he sent his Son to be our sin substitute.

The better we are able to accept ourselves as God accepts us, the stronger and healthier our relationships and love bonds will be.

Attention is one way of saying to ourselves, *What do I feel and what do I need?* Not that we should put ourselves higher than anyone else, but we should give thought to which feelings and needs are not being met and why.

As women we're especially good at scolding ourselves and thinking about what we should have done. But how many of us are good at empathizing or comforting ourselves, or letting the Lord comfort us? We could begin by telling ourselves, *I've really had a long hard day and it's okay to feel a little blue tonight. Maybe I should treat myself tenderly and make something easy for dinner instead of the big meal I usually cook.* When we begin to practice empathy with ourselves, it's amazing how that empathy spills over onto others.

It is nice to receive support and encouragement from others, but it's also sometimes important to "be your own best friend." I have clients tell me that they, at times, stop and ask themselves, *Now what would Dr. Shay say about this?* If they can't support themselves at first, I'm glad they stop to wonder what I would say. That's because I model good support and encouragement. Initially, they can own their personal solutions better if they think about what I would say in certain situations.

Eventually, however, they start thinking in those positive terms for themselves. Then it's their own thoughts and self-talk—what they know God says is true about them—that supports and encourages them.

How to Recognize Relational Bonding Needs

Fulfillment comes from bonding needs that are acknowledged and identified. Anger and frustration come from bonding needs that are not met.[2]

Understanding your own bonding needs also helps you to understand others. It's one of the keys to a good relationship. Sharing your relational needs with your spouse and giving him practical ways to meet that need can bring you closer together as a couple.

"Honey, I had a major conflict with my boss today. Can I share what happened with you and will you please empathize with me and listen? I'd rather you not try to fix it for me, but I really need your encouragement right now."

> My number one bonding need is attention from my husband.

Understanding your husband's top few intimacy needs can also help you know how to love and support him. Think of the insight you could gain into your relationship if you sought to understand why each of you has your particular bonding needs.

My number one bonding need is attention from my husband. We both work outside the house, so when I come home I like Bob to be as interested in my day as I am in his. Because my father was a workaholic and we rarely had much father-daughter time, I may have a deficit in the area of a loved one's attention.

Bob, on the other hand, doesn't need as much attention as I do, but he does crave appreciation. I have had to practice noticing all the things he accomplishes and commenting on how much I appreciate them. Since I don't need appreciation as much as he does, I had to train myself to notice and comment, just as he had to realize I need more face-to-face time with him in the evenings than he needs with me.

Stages of Bonding

I've observed five stages of bonding that occur as a couple moves from courting to attachment. A healthy relationship takes time to grow. We've seen many problems in relationships because the couple rushed into marriage when they weren't even through stage one of emotional connection.

The Bible uses the word "wait" more than 150 times, often referring to one's relationship with God. So I surmise that if, at times, God wants us to wait in our relationship with him, he also created human bonding to have times of waiting and moving slowly. Particularly, we should not rush into marriage or sexuality.

Stage one is the stage where everyone looks nice, acts nice, and smells nice. It's a superficial stage—the "getting to know you" stage. Since opposite personalities attract, we usually pick someone who has an opposite temperament. If the man is outgoing and talkative, he may be attracted to the introverted, good listener. We seem to look for a partner with some of the qualities we may lack. But while opposite temperaments may attract, everything else that can be alike should be for optimal relationship success. This includes backgrounds, interests, religions, values, ideas on marriage and family, etc. This is the stage where a woman can identify if she has picked someone who fits her "lovemap" and whether following the lovemap is good or bad for her, depending on her early life relationships. As tragic as it is, many women with alcoholic fathers marry alcoholic husbands, oblivious to the lovemap pattern.

Stage two is when we begin to identify similar interests, and let our guard down a little. We feel more comfortable with the other person and begin to share our life stories. We may meet each other's friends and see how we all fit in. This is a good time to look for consistency in the other person. Does what he says match up with what he does? Having integrity involves acting in a way that is consistent with our stated values. Integrity is being the same on the outside as we are on the inside.

This is also a good time to meet each other's families and watch how the other interacts with his or her mother, father, and siblings. Any unresolved issues between your partner and his mother or father will be brought into the marriage and laid at your feet. At times people project onto their partners the behaviors they saw in one of their parents. So if a man's mother was unfaithful in the marriage relationship with the father, this new male interest may think you're flirting when you look around and smile at someone in a restaurant—which, of course, is not true at all. Or a man with a controlling mother may unconsciously think all women are controlling and may see you as controlling, even if you aren't. Stage two is a good time to take stock of the situation intelligently and not hide your head in the infatuation sand.

Stage three occurs when we have watched this person long enough to truly trust him. We begin to be more vulnerable. We may share our hopes and dreams. We may evaluate his spiritual walk and his moral and ethical value system, as well as checking out our own. How does he follow through, manage his money, and respect our boundaries? These behaviors will become very important later on, so be alert for any red flags now.

Can you be yourself with this person? Does he try to change you or fix you? On the other hand, are you thinking you can *change* him? Does he invalidate your feelings by basically telling you to get over it? Do you get the feeling you may not ever measure up to his standards?

The time to address these problems is before you walk down the aisle. People are more motivated to change before the wedding than after. However, make sure the change stays consistent for at least a year. People can be deceptive for a while, but it's hard to keep up a pretense for over a year.

Stage four is when the relationship is closing in on oneness. It begins with what I call the leaving and cleaving process. We may be more affectionate and start to dream and talk about our life together. Phrases like "when we get married" and "once we buy a house" crop up more and more. We become known as a couple and our families are waiting for the engagement announcement. It's still not too late to keep evaluating, so we keep our eyes open and pray for discernment about the relationship. Consistency is still the key.

Is the person consistent with what you know about him over time? Are your families both thrilled about the growing oneness? Have you talked about premarital counseling with your pastor or therapist and is your loved one willing to go? If a man balks at this, he may have something to hide. Remember, even engagement is a time of continued evaluation of the relationship.

Stage five is the ultimate statement of commitment from both parties. We have watched this person over time and are convinced that God's blessing will be on this marriage. We are as sure of this person's integrity as we are of our own. We feel absolutely certain we are not settling for mediocrity or a counterfeit but have waited for God's best. The natural outgrowth of this stage is marriage and sexuality, which we will deal with in more depth in the following chapters.

Bonding in a female is crucial to her later sexuality. Too often women have jumped from stage one of bonding (superficiality) to stage five (marriage and sexuality), thinking the three stages in the middle are not important. But once you reach marriage and sexuality, it's very difficult to go back and pick up the three bonding stages you lost.

Points to Consider

1. We all have bonding needs.
2. Bonding needs are meant to be met by God, ourselves, and our mates, as well as by family and friends.
3. We need to love ourselves just as God loves us.
4. Fulfillment comes from bonding needs that are acknowledged and identified. Anger and frustration come from bonding needs that are not met.
5. The five stages of bonding are getting to know the other person, identifying similar traits, evaluation and trust, leaving and cleaving, and committment.
6. Stages of bonding take time and need to be worked through consecutively for a healthy relationship to build.

CHAPTER 3

Is It Dependency or Is It Love?

There is only one sort of love,
but a thousand copies.

François de La Rochefoucauld

It was a complaint I'd heard many times before. My new client, Candy, told me, "My mother is my big problem. She calls and tells me what to do and I can't argue with her or have a different viewpoint because I think it might hurt her. I feel guilty and selfish if I don't agree with her."

I asked what would happen if she did disagree with her mother.

"If I disagreed, my mother would say, 'I can't believe you're so disrespectful to your mother. Why, I might die tomorrow and then what would you do? You're a selfish and ungrateful girl! When I think of all I've done for you I can't believe how mean you're being.' "

I asked Candy if she believed what her mother said.

Candy's voice became a whisper as she said, "Sort of. My fear is that Mom might really die or punish me by staying angry and never calling me."

At a subsequent session Candy revealed a similar problem with her husband. "My husband isn't considerate of my feelings and is always giving me things to do at the last minute. It's like he doesn't think I have a life of my own! I'm afraid he'll get mad if I say 'no' or 'not now,' especially when he wants sex."

I replied, "What is your greatest fear if he did get mad?"

She tearfully replied, "That he'd leave me."

Over time Candy began to realize that maybe this was more than just a family problem; it also extended to others outside the family.

"I was really trying to make friends with this certain girl at work. I began to see that I was giving in to her way of doing things, even though I was the supervisor. It became evident that she was losing respect for me and expecting preferential treatment."

Candy saw how she had lost control at work, and we discussed some ways to get it back. I wondered out loud to Candy if this pattern could be affecting another supervisory position—motherhood. She admitted she felt too permissive with her kids, just like she felt with her coworker. One of the reasons she immediately gave in was because she felt guilty, that she didn't spend enough time with them and feared their anger and criticism.

In a follow-up session I gave Candy some insight into the fact that her permissiveness was another facet of the same problem.

Finally she asked, "Dr. Shay, how do I undo this pattern?"

This was a good starting point for investigating the difference between dependency and love. It's evident that Candy's confusion, guilt, and anger, all converged to give her the feeling that her life was upside down. She was not displaying love; she was displaying self-protection based on the anxiety (future-oriented threat) of abandonment, rejection, and criticism. I helped her understand that saying no to her mother wouldn't *hurt* her mother, but it might *disappoint* her. Everyone faces disappointment sometimes and there are no exceptions to this rule. She wasn't responsible to rescue her mother from every disappointment. But she was responsible to God to be honest since she admitted there were many times when she said yes when she wanted to say no.

We explored how the fear of her husband's potential anger—when he was told "no" or "not now" about sex—only made Candy angry. Yet, she suppressed that anger and let it smolder. Suppressed anger turns into bitterness, then resentment, and over time could bring Candy to the point where she didn't want to have sex at all with her husband.

Trying to win someone's approval by not being true to yourself, your feelings, and your needs always ends in disaster. Although Candy's motives sounded good, they really were emotionally unfulfilling for her and the people she loved. The internalized anger was a loaded gun.

Candy had a major difficulty—she couldn't say no to anyone. While trying to be everything to everyone, she ended up having problems with everybody. Candy actually was dependent on her mother, husband, coworker, and even her children for their approval. She couldn't say no to any of them for fear of the negative repercussions—disapproval, rejection, and real or imagined abandonment. Her major issue was one of dependency.

Dependency is a problem of emotional limits or boundaries. A dependent person has no emotional borders between themselves and others. Even if a person has some boundaries, many times they don't feel valuable enough to respect what lies within their own emotional borders. Emotional limits help you have the freedom to have your own thoughts, opinions, and emotions. They help you understand what you say no to and what you say yes to. They can also help you disconnect from the harmful, manipulative emotions of others. This was one skill that Candy needed to learn in relation to everyone in her life.

Candy viewed mistakes as failures instead of seeing them as learning opportunities. Children who are shamed for mistakes are being kept dependent and needy by receiving the message from the parents that they cannot do anything without them.

How Dependency Develops

Candy wanted to know how and when dependency begins and ends. How could she, as an adult, grow past unhealthy dependency? I explained that while some specific stages of boundaries could be seen at different ages, boundary development was a lifelong process.

In their excellent book, *The Psychological Birth of the Human Infant,* Mahler, Pine, and Bergman explain: "The biological birth of the human infant and the psychological birth of the individual are not coincident (concurrent) in time. The former is a dramatic, observable, and well-circumscribed event; the latter a slowly unfolding process."[1] So our psychological birth takes time and goes through certain stages.

If a young girl is allowed to break away and given responsibility in small things at a regular slow rate, she will usually end up a healthy young woman with confidence and good judgment. A healthy parent is always backpedaling out of their child's life—five percent at a time—and cheering them for every good decision while helping them learn from the poor ones. Jesus never yelled, shamed, or withdrew from anyone to discipline them. He taught with love, limits, and consequences.

Look over the following stages and see how you would rate your own "individuation," or breaking away from dependency. The following stages were developed by Mahler, Pine, and Bergman. Dr. Henry Cloud and Dr. John Townsend also have written extensively on boundaries and the stages of individuation and some of their concepts are included as well in the following discussion.

Stage One: Symbiosis

Symbiosis means "a relationship of dependence." This is the state of a baby depending on her mother. In this first stage, the baby thinks she is the same as the mother. This stage lasts until approximately four to five months of age.

Stage Two: Differentiation Stage

Differentiation occurs between five and ten months of age. The baby begins to realize she is not Mom. She is separate from Mom and wants to learn about life through every sense. That's why babies put everything in their mouths, reach for anything their little eyes can see, and pull away from the breast or bottle at the slightest noise. They want to explore and discover. They are still dependent on their mother, but they aren't so enraptured with her.

New mothers may feel slighted, but this development is a good sign because those early nurturing months have given the baby the security to start to reach out and discover the world.

Sometimes women who never fully went through the differentiation stage for themselves can miss the closeness and dependency of those early months of symbiosis with their baby. Once the total dependency stage wears off, they want another child who will be completely dependent upon them again. Candy's mother had told her she had nursed until she was three years old and was a very compliant child. Candy was her mother's "constant companion." Possibly, her mother had not encouraged any independence and needed Candy's dependency to meet her own needs.

Stage Three: Practicing Stage

From ten months to eighteen months a baby is in the practicing stage where transportation and speech are very important. While a baby who is differentiating can look around and crawl away, a baby in the practicing stage can run and talk while they are doing it! These toddlers feel energetic, impulsive, and curious, wanting to try any new thing that they think of. Walking and talking gives them a sense of invincibility as they try new things.

When my son was one year old he took a butter knife off the table and was headed right for the light socket. The evening before I had been wallpapering, and he had seen me take the light socket cover off the wall with a knife. I hadn't realized how astute and fast he'd become! Thankfully, I caught him in time.

As I taught these stages to Candy, she said in a small, frightened voice, "I didn't walk until fifteen months. Mother said I was a shy child preferring to stay home with her than going to preschool or kindergarten. I guess that's why I hated first grade. I never learned to be confident in myself. I was so scared being away from Mom, I cried all the time."

I explained that boundaries could be learned in adulthood even if they were not taught in early childhood. Knowing these stages would help her understand her own and other's dependency issues. This awareness could help her rely on God's unconditional, constant love during times of boundary setting. Knowing God would never leave or forsake her was of great comfort to her through her therapy.

Stage Four: Rapprochement Stage

God has designed these stages to be consecutive in preparing the child to be ready for the next stage. The practicing stage gives way for the rapprochement stage to begin. Rapprochement really means "a reinstatement or reestablishment of pleasant/cordial relations" with the parents. The child begins to realize she can't do everything she wants and still needs Mom's help. This reconnecting to mother is different this time because the child now brings a sense of "self" into the relationship.[2] The child is now separate with her own feelings and desires. She begins to express herself as an individual by using anger, ownership, and the word *no*.

Toddlers need choices and options, not just yes and no questions. "Would you like to wear your red shorts?" most likely will get a no answer. "Would you like to wear the red or blue shorts?" is a better question, giving the child a sense of some control while you stack the deck by giving two good choices. Then it's important to praise the child for a good decision. In this way you develop in the child a sense of confidence in her ability to be independent and make good choices. She also feels her mother's happiness at her budding independence.

Some parents punish children for independence, thus encouraging unnecessary dependence. Later in life, dependents gravitate to other controllers who punish them for independence.

Ironically, Candy's sister Beth had similar dependency issues. Beth had married a very controlling man who punished her with silence and withdrawal anytime she wanted simply to go out with Candy for a lunch or dinner date.

If a child hasn't gone through these stages of "leaving and then cleaving again" she may feel insecure, unsure of her own judgments, and scared to face life without a strong voice to direct her.

Two other ages when people learn to break dependency and set boundaries are adolescence and young adulthood. During adolescence it's important to set limits of morality and ethics, modesty, legality, and spiritual concepts, but it's also important to allow the adolescent to make choices within those limits. So if a teen wants to wear baggy jeans and it isn't against the dress code at her school, or isn't immoral, immodest, or illegal, allowing her to wear the jeans helps her individuate by making choices for herself. Conversely, if the parent dictates exactly what she should wear, the teen stays dependent and is at risk of not individuating.

When teens begin dating, parents need to strike that delicate balance:

- Setting boundaries without imposing control
- Building trust without compromising parental authority
- Giving them a gradually increasing measure of freedom without becoming too permissive[3]

As you would expect by now, Candy was the "perfect" child who never had differing opinions from Mom. "Mom was my best friend," she said. "I just thought she knew everything so it never dawned on me to disagree with her." As an adult Candy was still agreeing with everyone and building up anger and resentment—the two by-products of dependency.

When young adults leave home for college or career they have a great deal of freedom. If you have allowed them to individuate slowly and methodically, they will be ready to face the numerous decisions that will be coming their way. If, however, the parent has made the young adult dependent by making most of her decisions, she will be overwhelmed by the freedom. She will either continue to allow the parents to dictate her life, get out of control like a dog off a leash heading for trouble, or transfer her dependency to someone more controlling, yet who lacks the love and commitment of the parent.

Candy went right from living at home while she attended the local college to meeting her husband and marrying him the day after graduation. She went from one "Mom" to another since he picked up where Mom left off in directing and controlling her. A great deal of unresolved anger and smoldering resentment continued to grow.

Allowing a child to "individuate," to begin to become an individual, starts very young and is not fully completed until young adulthood. It is the healthy opposite to damaging dependency. Individuation has three main distinctions.

1. Individuated people have good emotional borders and retain a sense of self. They can be emotionally attached to others but still be apart without anxiety, anger, fear, guilt, or sadness. They don't lose themselves in a relationship by practically becoming the other person. If two people are exactly the same, one of them is unnecessary.
2. They can say no when it is appropriate and not worry about manipulation, disappointment, the other person's anger, pity, or false guilt.

3. They can allow other people to say no to them and not try to convince or manipulate them into saying yes. They are able to take no for an answer and be okay with it.[4]

You may wonder why a book on female sexuality is going over developmental stages of childhood, but the truth is that many women have never been allowed or encouraged to fully develop beyond dependency into a healthy adult with boundaries and emotional limits. If a woman has no emotional limits she is dependent on others for approval. The by-product of dependency is suppressed anger and resentment.

In my observation of women, unresolved anger is one of the leading psychological blocks to wanting intimacy with her spouse. Addressing this deep issue is foundational to dealing with any other sexual problems.

Dangers of Dependency

A person with dependency issues is like a half person. That half person finds another half person and she believes that two halves will make a whole. Even controlling spouses or parents are really as dependent as the dependent person they manipulate. They, too, want someone else to make them whole.

However, God's plan was for us to mature in him, to become a strong individual, and to want a whole partner instead of needing a half partner. A young, single physician with whom I worked on dependency issues said it best, "I wasted too much time with those half girls. Now I want a whole woman because now I'm a whole man!"

Signs of Dependency in a Relationship

- Initiating most of the calls and times spent together.
- Talking about the relationship more than the other person does.
- Feeling anxiety when not with the partner a great deal. Angry when the partner wants alone time or time with friends.
- Unwilling to voice disagreement with the partner's plans or feelings for fear of rejection or disapproval.
- Unhappy when the other seems perfectly fine when they're not together.
- Wanting to know everything the other person does, thinks, and feels.
- Feeling indecisive and unable to make decisions without the other's reassurance. Feeling crushed or devastated with other's criticism.
- Carrying a disproportionate responsibility for the relationship.
- Feeling helpless and constantly needing reassurance for fear the relationship will end.

The Litmus Test of Love

Now that we know what we don't want, lets look at what we do want, genuine love. The kind of love God intended for us. In his wisdom, God gave us a litmus test to see what real love looks like. The following is my paraphrase of 1 Corinthians 13:

Love is patient, kind, and never gives up.
Love is polite, unselfish, and tolerant.
Love appreciates what it has.

Love is humble and receives compliments graciously.
Love asks for permission to cross boundaries.
Love loves others as much as it loves itself.
Love is disciplined and uses self-control.
Love is tolerant and forbearing with others' weaknesses and challenges.
Love has true compassion and empathy.
Love takes pleasure in respect and truth.
Love is always loyal.
Love trusts God at all times.
Love always looks for the best.
Love keeps going to the end.

Real love is found in the larger ideas revealed in 1 Corinthians 13, but it's also in the little things that sometimes go overlooked.

- Giving genuine praise in front of others
- Placing people before things
- Listening instead of tying to fix things
- Celebrating special occasions
- Promoting win-win outcomes from every argument
- Both people saying "I'm sorry"
- Knowing the partner's intimacy needs and seeking to meet them
- Being patient, praying about things before bringing them up
- Examining your expectations and discussing them
- Allowing your partner to grow
- Praying together every day for your marriage

The chart that follows compares love and dependency.

LOVE	DEPENDENCY
Love is patient, kind, and never gives up.	Dependency is impatient, wants immediate gratification.
Love is polite, unselfish, and tolerant.	Dependency is anxious and wants its own way.
Love appreciates what it has.	Dependency always wants more.
Love is humble and receives compliments graciously.	Dependency is always looking for reassurance.
Love asks for permission to cross boundaries.	Dependency is anxious and desperate to connect, even if boundaries are crossed.
Love loves self and others.	Dependency is unhappy when the other loves self.
Love is disciplined and uses self-control.	Dependency is frantic and impulsive to get needs met.
Love is liberal and forbearing with others' weaknesses and challenges.	Dependency seems empathetic but unconsciously harbors resentment.
Love has true compassion and empathy.	Dependency is giving empathy to get love.
Love takes pleasure in respect and truth.	Dependency is unable to truly respect itself.
Love is always loyal.	Dependency is loyal to protecting itself.
Love trusts God at all times.	Dependency fears abandonment from everyone.
Love always looks for the best.	Dependency frets about the worst.
Love keeps going to the end.	Dependency will jump ship if a better situation comes along.

As you can see, dependency can masquerade as love until we look at the motivation that precedes the action. Is the motivation the joy of loving or the protection of self out of the fear of rejection and abandonment?

The Components of Love

In *The Pursuit of Intimacy,* Ferguson and Thurmond describe the three equal parts of love: *desirability/attraction, intimacy,* and *commitment.*

We've discussed desirability/attraction in depth in chapter one. What, then, is intimacy? The word *intimacy* comes from the Latin word *intimus*, which means innermost. It can be a desire for emotional, physical, and spiritual closeness or connectedness. It involves knowing someone thoroughly and accepting them unconditionally. I define it this way:

Intimacy is the vulnerability to be 100 percent honest with another person while speaking the truth in love, without fear of anger, shame, criticism, or rejection.

Intimacy involves our body, soul, and spirit. Genesis 2:7 says, "God formed man's *body* from the dust of the ground and breathed into him the *spirit* of life, and he became a living *soul.*" Think of it this way:

Body = Sexual closeness; resembling *eros,* sensual love
Soul = Friendship; *phileo,* love with our mind, will, and emotions
Spirit = Spiritual fellowship; *agape* love; Jesus' selfless love

Intimacy problems can occur in any of these areas. One relationship can boast a great sex life but have no real friendship or spiritual depth. Another marriage can have close spiritual intimacy, mediocre friendship, but no sexual attraction.

The goal of a healthy *loving, not dependent, relationship* is to have thriving spiritual closeness, great sexual fulfillment, and the enjoyment of being married to your best friend.[5]

Husbands and Wives Can Keep Each Other Happy with Just Fifteen Little Words

"I love you."
"Let's eat out."
"Can I help?"
"It's my fault."
"You look fabulous."

Commitment is the third component of love. Commitment is a state of being emotionally, intellectually, and spiritually bound to another person. A commitment is expressed in a covenant, a vow, or a promise. When we enter into the marriage covenant, we vow to love, honor, and cherish the other partner—and we make that promise to God as well.

When my husband and I counsel a troubled couple together, we give them a shorthand version of the marriage vows and ask them to say them out loud to each other every day.

A Marriage Vow

I will love you when things are wonderful or awful,
I will honor you always,
I will cherish you even if we are in conflict,
I will never be disloyal to you,
And I promise this forever
So help me God.

I like the idea of a "mission statement" for love. Some I've read incorporate several good ideas:

WE WILL BE INTIMATE FIRST WITH GOD AND THEN EACH OTHER. WE WILL GIVE PRIORITY TO OUR NEEDS AND THE NEEDS OF OUR LOVED ONE. OUR UNION WILL ALWAYS BE OUR PRIORITY, TRUSTING EACH OTHER WITH OUR INNERMOST SELVES.

Or,

WE WILL SEEK TO COMMIT TO GOD AND EACH OTHER OUR BODIES, MINDS, AND SPIRITS. WE WILL ACCEPT AND LOVE EACH OTHER UNCONDITIONALLY. WE WILL BE VULNERABLE WITHOUT FEAR. WE WILL SEEK TO KEEP OUR COMMUNICATION OPEN AND TRUE.

Reminding ourselves of these promises strengthens our commitment and thus, our love. How often has a child begged and pleaded to take ballet, piano, or karate lessons only to get bored or disinterested at some point and want to quit? Poor follow-through and giving up easily are characteristics of childhood and immaturity. A wise person realizes that loving commitment takes discipline and perseverance, even more so when the road is hard. Too often we "fall in love with love" and don't acknowledge that there will be bad times, times when we want to quit. My good friend, Father John Hyers, said it best when he quipped, "My wife and I have both wanted to quit at marriage; fortunately not at the same time."

Hopefully, through your life and through reading this chapter, you understand the difference between dependency and love. Love can grow from a dependent relationship. However, it takes awareness, prayer, and recognizing that God is the only one who ultimately meets our need for approval and acceptance.

My prayer is that you will be motivated to evaluate all your relationships, firm up the boundaries, speak the truth in love without fear of rejection or abandonment, and start loving yourself the way God loves you.

Points to Consider

1. Dependency is a problem with having no emotional limits or boundaries. A dependent person has no borders between themselves and others. They look to others for approval and affirmation.
2. Allowing children to individuate—to begin to become an individual—starts at a very young age and is not completed until young adulthood. It is the healthy opposite to damaging dependency.
3. Individuated people are not manipulated by other people's guilt, anger, or threats of abandonment. They can say no and they can be told no without fearing repercussions.
4. It is important to recognize the ten traits of dependency since the eventual by-product of dependency is anger and resentment.
5. Dependency is a cheap counterfeit for the real traits of love described in 1 Corinthians 13.
6. Love has three components: desirability, intimacy, and commitment.
7. Intimacy involves body, soul, and spirit.
8. Commitment is a covenant or promise both to God and to your mate.

9. Saying mini-vows to each other daily helps a marriage stay strong.
10. Developing a mission statement of love for a marriage helps keep a couple's goals in mind.

PART II

The Physiology of Sex

Gender Differences

We do not see things as they are;
we see things as we are.

Anaïs Nin

I enjoy humor that looks at the differences between men and women. I came across this dialogue and wanted to share it with you. God and Adam were having a discussion.

"God, why did you make Eve's hair so soft?"
"So you would love her, Adam."
"But why did you make her so curvy and pretty?"
"So you would love her, Adam."
"But God, why did you make her so forgiving?"
"So she would love YOU, Adam!"

I hope you won't mind my gentle gender teasing, but it's true—the sexes are different. Over the years in counseling hundreds of couples, my husband and I have made notes of some of the humorous differences between men and women and we've included ourselves.

1. Women think outside their heads and tend to externally process things. As women are talking they're also figuring out what they want. Men tend to process things internally. One morning at breakfast I said I was thinking about painting one of the living room walls navy blue. Bob heard my comment and made no reply. All through the day I changed that wall color fifteen times, trying on different colors in my mind. I finally decided wallpaper would be better. That evening, Bob walked in the door with rollers, pans, navy blue paint, drop cloths, and new paintbrushes. He thought I had definitely decided on painting the wall navy blue. Since Bob and many men process internally, he would never have mentioned a color until he had firmly decided he wanted the wall navy blue. Now Bob always asks me if I'm just processing outside my head or if I've come to a definite conclusion.

2. Often women seem in agreement with the things their husband says when, truthfully, they haven't made up their minds. A client named Teresa verbally agreed with her husband that they should add a room on the house. She wasn't really sure she wanted the extra room, but since she hadn't thought it over she went along with it. It wasn't until the construction company was on the way to the house that she thought it all the way through and decided she'd rather not build. Instead she told her husband that she'd rather look for a new house with all the things they really wanted. Her husband was furious, but I understood exactly. Teresa hadn't taken the time to think it through, and her husband assumed her easy com-

pliance was a hearty YES and proceeded full speed ahead. I'm not saying she was right, but women need to make themselves think things through before they go along with their husbands' plans.

3. Typically, a man has about ten to fifteen items in his side of the bathroom. They can include shaving cream, deodorant, razors, toothbrush and toothpaste, cologne, and possibly some skin care products. Most women have at least two hundred or more, counting all their makeup, hair care products, skin care products, etc. This same phenomena seems to apply to shoes as well. Whereas a man may have dress shoes in a couple colors, a pair or two of exercise shoes, dock shoes and sandals, many women have shoes to match almost every outfit they own. Another strange thing is that some women have up to ten pairs of black shoes. One of my client's husbands asked her to count her shoes. She estimated she had 60 pairs. When she made the actual count, she had 257 pairs of shoes.

4. Women tend to think emotionally; men tend to think logically. One of my clients looked lovingly into her husband's eyes and said, "We've been married six months, do you know what that means?" He responded, "Yes, and I'm glad you brought that up. We are three months overdue for an oil change in our new car."

5. Another difference occurs when men go to lunch with their friends. They talk about superficial things, laugh and joke, and even call each other nicknames. When the check arrives they all want to pay or all put in too much money and leave the waiter a big tip. When women go out to lunch they discuss the children, their feelings, sometimes their relationships, and rarely call each other nicknames. When the check arrives the most analytical in the group figures out what each one owes to the penny including a 15 percent tip and collects the right amount from each woman, leaving exact change.

6. Women know what day is "school spirit day" at their kids' school, which day the children want to buy or take their lunch, when their next big test is coming up, and how many days they have to finish the science project. Men are comfortable roughhousing on the floor with the kids and helping put them to bed, if they are asked.

7. Many women, if they are truthful, will admit they married their husband with a few things in mind they wanted to change about him. They're sadly disappointed when the changes don't occur.

Men, however, marry their wives hoping they will stay exactly as they were when they walked down the aisle. They are flabbergasted on their wedding night when the fake nails and eyelashes come off, the hairpiece is removed, and the Wonderbra® falls to the floor.

8. Women are gatherers and men are hunters. Women, looking for a silk blouse, will go to every store in a mall, try on numerous silk blouses, and compare the prices before making a purchase. Men will walk in the first store closest to where they parked, find the right sized polo shirt, buy it, and leave before his wife has even ordered her caffe latte.

9. Men will stare intently at a sporting event, and then become upset if their wives accidentally step in front of the TV. However, that same man will never relinquish the remote control to anyone else in the family, and during commercials, channel surf other stations, causing his wife to miss the best part of her show or movie.

10. Women and men frequently interpret the same sentence in different ways. One man came up to his wife, winked, and said, "Why don't we try swapping positions tonight?" "Great!" she replied. "You cook dinner, clean up, put the kids to bed, and I'll lie on the couch and click the remote control."

Some of the differences between men and women can be quite comical. Believe it or not, God made us different, not to make our lives difficult, but to complement each other. Since both men and women are made in God's image, our maleness and femaleness display the different aspects of God's character. God can be just, powerful, and trusted, while also being the epitome of compassion and love. My friend, Pastor Randy Evans of Grace Christian Fellowship in Largo, Florida, elaborates:

> We see in the nature, character, and behavior of our Lord God a whole array of fatherly, paternal instincts. Our Father God is a God of authority. He is one who can be trusted; he is faithful and attentive; he is affectionate and accepting—all traits that we would hope to find in an earthly father.
>
> But our Lord God is also the perfect mother and we shouldn't be embarrassed or afraid to say that. He's the ultimate Mr. Mom. His compassionate, exquisitely loving side can be seen in Isaiah 49:15, 16: "Can a mother forget the baby at her breast and have no compassion on the child she has borne? Though she may forget, I will not forget you! See, I have engraved (tattooed) you on the palms of my hands; your walls are ever before me."
>
> What this verse tells us about mothers (and the maternal characteristics of God) is that their child—no matter how old—will always be in their mind. They won't forget about their child. This speaks of a motherly devotion and loyalty that far exceeds what we would normally see in the world among other relationships. Most relationships are fair-weather relationships. The moment trouble comes they run as far away from the person and problem as they can. Not so with a mother. A mother's love is different than any other kind of love.

Surely our gender differences reflect the different characteristics of God. This isn't to say that men can't love tenderly and women can't be authoritative and strong. Rather, the key is that gender differences were created by God to reflect God's own personality, particularly as they complement each other in a loving marital relationship.

You may feel the following differences listed are a generalization and don't hold true for you and your spouse. You may find that you and your husband exhibit traits from both lists. Both responses are valid. Gender difference lists aren't written in stone; these are simply observations that my husband and I have made over the years of working with many types of people with sexual problems.

Understanding these common (but not exhaustive) differences is helpful for understanding our mates, our sons, our fathers, and our male friends.

Sexual Differences Between Men and Women

MEN	WOMEN
1. Need appreciation and respect	1. Need to be valued by husband's love and attention. Love is spelled t-i-m-e.
2. Visually stimulated	2. Tactilely stimulated—sex begins with nonsexual affection
3. Men want action	3. Women want relationship
4. Men want more frequency	4. Women want less frequency

1. Men Need Appreciation; Women Need Attention

The observation that men are more likely to need appreciation and respect, while women need more attention and love is clearly reflected in what God himself commanded in Ephesians 5:33: "However, each one of you must also love his wife as he loves himself and the wife must respect her husband." Love goes hand in hand with attention and respect goes hand in hand with appreciation. Many of the women I see who complain of not being loved make these types of statements:

"He won't take out the trash."	EQUALS "He doesn't care about me."
"He leaves me alone at parties."	EQUALS "He doesn't pay attention to me."
"He just vegges out with the TV."	EQUALS "He doesn't connect with me."
"He thinks I'm fat."	EQUALS "He doesn't think I'm sexy anymore."

These are all statements from women who feel unloved—they are not histrionic, selfish, or attention seeking. They may just genuinely want to feel connected to their husbands and need their men to convey some love, interest, and time to them. How will these men know this? Women can express to their husbands exactly what they need and, sometimes, even tell them how to say it. Explain how it makes you feel when your husband says:

"You look so fantastic in that dress I won't think of anything else all day." Clarify the words that really compliment you.

"When you bent over the stove I thought how gorgeous your legs are in those shorts." These words begin putting a woman in the mood for lovemaking knowing she's noticed and admired.

Teach your husband to recognize your intelligence and maturity as well as complimenting your physical body. Coach your husband on observing and commenting on situations where your acumen shows. "I was very impressed by your input when we were discussing politics with Linda and Mike," is a positive compliment that will ring in your ears long after the event has passed.

Many men did not grow up with fathers who knew how to love their mothers. A godly husband will be grateful to learn what helps meet your foundational needs, instead of just having to guess. Women's magazines are forever telling women how to be sexy and romantic, but when was the last time you saw an article in a men's magazine on romance?

By lovingly speaking the truth, communicate to your husband that his affirmation of you for your looks, intelligence, and godly characteristics makes you feel loved, emotionally supported, and attended to. Encourage him:

- to truthfully inquire about your day,
- to notice you,
- to offer positive feedback and validation to you.

This will meet your need for attention and genuine love—and you'll be able to respond to his physical expressions of love. Love begets love and it starts a cycle that goes on and on and on.

Many women are offended by the way men focus on the woman's body. We want to be appreciated and accepted for our minds, talents, achievements, and abilities. We want to be thought of as not just a body, but as a whole person—body, mind, and soul.

My husband, Dr. Bob Roop, reminds me that sometimes it's just the opposite for a man. He says men are tired of being told they are wonderful husbands, fathers, and providers. They'd just like to be sex objects *once in awhile.* Information he has gathered from years of working with men regarding sexuality suggests that men would love to have their wives focus on their bodies and their virility. For example in one man's session the client stated, "Women say they hate to be leered at by construction workers but if the girls at the bank want to peer over their counters and whistle as I walk in, they can just tell me a time and I'll be there."

As humorous as that is, men also need positive feedback about their physical characteristics. Men love to be complimented on their masculinity or why would they spend so much time at the gym pumping iron? Women tend to compliment other women about their hair or new dress, but men rarely rave over each other's haircut, their new tie, or their waistline. Men like to hear kind words about their physical appearance as much as women do because men get so little of it anywhere else.

The most frequent comment made by men is that their wives don't respect or appreciate them, especially in the bedroom. Every woman knows that it isn't the man who gives them an orgasm—but the man sure does help the process along. A man feels appreciated, respected, and masculine when a woman is aroused sexually and has a significant orgasm. Telling your husband, "Thanks for last night—that was mind-blowing" is like giving him intravenous self-esteem. He needs to know you appreciate everything he does, but appreciating his sexual prowess is like catnip to the cat.

Let's face it, most men will never be pro golfers, win the Kentucky Derby, or become president. But if a man knows he can make the earth move for his wife, he will walk a little taller, feel more masculine, and love her even better for it. *Praising a man to success* is more productive and yields better results than *criticizing him to success.* More people are prone to change with positive reinforcement than negative reinforcement.

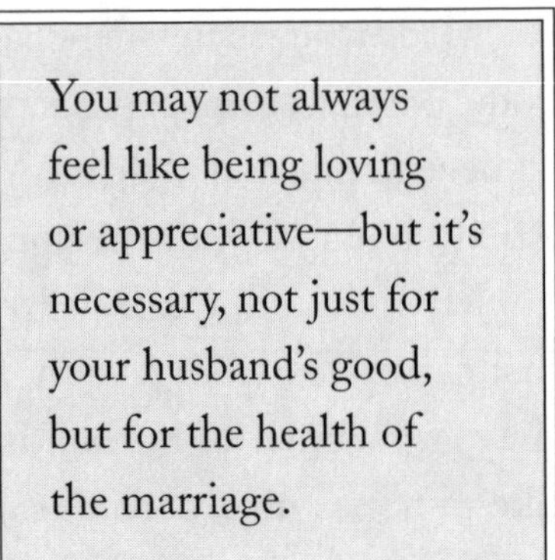
You may not always feel like being loving or appreciative—but it's necessary, not just for your husband's good, but for the health of the marriage.

This means that if you make your needs known to your husband and he tries to meet that need in the smallest way, make a big deal about it, thank him repeatedly, and he will be much more apt to do it again in a bigger way. If you wait to praise him until everything is exactly right, he may become demotivated and give up.

Three women who felt as if they weren't getting their "attention needs" met were having lunch and complaining about their husbands. An attractive younger man came up to one of them and whispered in her ear, "I'll do anything, absolutely anything, for fifty dollars."

The woman thought a minute, took a fifty-dollar bill from her purse and slipped it into his hand saying, "Clean my house."

Women certainly can experience love in a different way than men.

2. Men Are Visually Stimulated; Women Are Tactilely Stimulated

The second difference between genders is vitally important for sexuality. Men are visually stimulated and have a continuing desire for release. Studies show they think about sex many more times in a day than women do. It's like their gun is loaded, ready to shoot, and a visual stimulus gives them an itchy trigger finger. The female gun, however, is still in the holster, or better yet, locked in a drawer or on the back shelf of the attic closet. Very few women are aroused simply by looking at a man's naked body. Not that they don't love the muscular build, hairy chest, wide shoulders, or handsome face, but visual stimuli typically do not turn on women. It may be "eye candy," but it doesn't get the ignition switch cranked.

Women are tactile or more stimulated by touch. Touch helps a woman start to connect with her senses and relax. That's why it is best to start any sexual encounter with nonsexual touch. When a man goes right for a woman's erogenous zones she feels rushed and can't relax. Then she tells herself, *I'll never have an orgasm at this rate.* Relaxed touching helps a woman to begin picturing the gun in her closet, to feel like getting it down, and finally, loading it.

One man commented that he made love by "running around the bases and hitting a home run." First base was a kiss, second base was a minute or two of breast touching, third base was a little genital touching, and the home run was insertion and ejaculation. He thought sex was a baseball game and speed was what won him the game. Sadly, he struck out with his wife because he missed her greatest sexual need—slow tactile stimulation.

The baseball player's wife wanted a man with a slow gentle demeanor. This is what she wrote when asked to describe the exact foreplay she would like: "I want John to first kiss me gently and then build up to more sensuous kissing. Then I want him to kiss my breasts and touch them with his tongue, and then come back to kissing my mouth. I'd like him to begin rubbing my arms and legs. Up and down my arms and chest, then up and down my legs and then gently stroke my genitals. I'd like him to rotate among kissing my mouth, my breasts, touching my genitals and rubbing my body. This sort of teases me and gets me turned on. I like him to touch me a little and then back up to kissing me, building up my anticipation of being touched again."

A woman needs time to catch up with a man since it takes her longer to get turned on. Most women would love to start sex with a back rub (or front rub without genital touching) so she can get as turned on as her spouse is. It's an old but true adage—WOMEN ARE CROCK-POTS, MEN ARE MICROWAVES.

Women have different needs in sex and it's important to communicate those needs. You can explain your needs and desires verbally, or in a letter if you're shy, but your husband needs to know how he can get you as aroused as he is.

3. Men Want Action; Women Want Relationship

John Eldredge in *Wild at Heart* writes, "The secret longing of a man's heart . . . is to explore, build, conquer; you don't have to tell a boy to do those things for the simple reason that it is his purpose."[1]

Men tend to think of life as a destination and especially so with sex. More men tend to be goal oriented and are hunters, exploring and conquering. Their buildup of sexual tension is strong and, naturally, they want release. They have the ability to get quickly aroused and erect, and then ejaculate typically with no problems.

Women are more relational and like to connect on an emotional and tactile level. When my clients talk about "girls' night out" it usually involves eating at a nice restaurant so they can catch up on each others' lives. They tend to compliment each other at different times through the evening and then hug good-bye. It has been said that women speak 25,000 words a day; men speak 12,500. Women see life as a journey that they want to savor and discuss as they go along.

Women like to talk, connect, and have some romance before intimacy. For women sex literally begins in the kitchen, not in the bedroom. Women need to teach their husbands that they want to feel some consideration and connection all day long before they desire sexual closeness at night. Most women want to discuss the day's events with their husband, have some nonsexual affection, and hear some compliments before they are ready for sex.

4. Men Want More Frequency; Women Want Less

The most commonly asked question that I hear is:

> "Am I normal? We have sex ___ times a week and I'm not sure we are normal."

A classic study, *The Social Organization of Sexuality: Sex in America,* found that:

> One-third of Americans have sex two or more times a week.
> One-third of Americans have sex one time in two weeks.
> One-third of Americans have sex a few times/year or none at all.[2]

You can see that there is a wide range in sexual frequency. Frequency is only a problem if you or your spouse requests more or less sex. If you are both happy with your own personal frequency, then that is what is *normal* for you.

Many women are uncomfortable saying no to their spouse for fear that their spouse will end up cheating on them, turn to pornography as an outlet, or ultimately, withdraw from them emotionally. One of the largest surveys done regarding men's sexuality was *The Hite Report* where seven thousand men were polled about infidelity. Surveys show that 40 to 50 percent of men who have been married have been unfaithful. Among women who have been married and yet have been unfaithful, the range is 10 to 30 percent.

But in a recent poll done by the Kinsey Institute, it showed that the average woman thinks that 70 percent of men cheat on their wives. It would *appear* that women may think men have more affairs than they actually do.[3]

A woman needs to learn to say "not now" instead of "no." This lets her husband know she is willing, but not at that exact moment. Here are some reasons why:

Men tell us that sexual rejection is one major reason they sometimes lose interest in sex. They feel as if they have been rejected so much that it is easier not to ask anymore. Sexual rejection is one of a man's most sensitive and vulnerable areas.

Intellectually, they understand we women might not be in the mood, but emotionally they personalize our rejection. "She doesn't want sex," becomes "she doesn't want sex *with me.*"

Men think about sex more than women, usually once or more a day. Because they want it so much more, they feel more rejected when they do not get it.

Let's look in on a woman who knows how to say no with love.

JIM: "I feel frisky tonight."

SUE THINKS TO HERSELF: *Oh no! Not tonight! I still have to make Laura's costume, take Steve to get new shoes, and finish a resume for my new position. Why not last night? I was rested, bathed, and in the mood—and he was watching the ball game.*

BUT SUE SAYS: "You know, you are the sexiest man I know and I can't get enough of you, but you caught me at a bad time tonight."

JIM THINKS TO HIMSELF: *Sue, Sue, Sue . . . telling me she can't get enough of me really made me feel good. Even if I end up having to delay our fun, she gave me a gift of acceptance and I don't feel personally rejected. She does sound pretty busy. I wonder if she needs my help.*

SO JIM SAYS: "Can I help you?"

SUE REPLIES: "I really could use your help and then maybe we can both get what we want. I'll finish this costume if you could take Steve to the mall for shoes. Then we can both get them to bed early and we can make a date for, say, 10 PM in our bedroom. You bring the candles and the music, and I'll bring the black teddy."

High Five!

First Corinthians 7 tells us that the wife's body belongs to the husband and the husband's body belongs to the wife. Verse five says, "Do not deprive each other except by mutual consent." Now some men might abuse that verse and say, "My wife ought to give herself to me whenever I want." But that attitude violates the other biblical commands of being kind one to another and being unselfish. It doesn't reflect true love which is patient and forbearing. Conversely, this is where truly loving your mate will encourage you to have sex sometimes even when you are not in the mood.

God made us different but he also made us intelligent enough to negotiate and compromise. By using his principles of kindness, consideration, and genuine love, many conflicts can end up win-win situations.

Points to Consider

1. Men need appreciation and respect, especially regarding their sexual prowess.
2. Women need attention from their husbands and it is spelled t-i-m-e.
3. Men think about sex many more times a day than women do.
4. Nonsexual touching helps a woman begin to relax and get in the mood for sex. She also typically needs twenty to thirty minutes of foreplay.
5. Women enjoy the journey and men like getting to the destination.
6. Women are Crock-Pots and men tend to be microwaves.
7. Both genders will have better communication and sexual happiness if they praise each other to success.
8. Since there are wide variations in frequency, "normal" is whatever frequency you and your mate agree upon and find acceptable.
9. Women can learn to let their husbands down easy by saying "not now" instead of a flat-out "no!"

Our Amazing Sexual Organs

No thing in life is to be feared.
It is to be understood.

Marie Curie

From the myriads of women in the world, each timeless and unique in her own beauty, God has devised an immense mosaic of womanhood. Though our personalities and experiences make us each so very different, all women have the same amazing sexual anatomy and the same basic sexual response. Psalm 139:13, 14 says, "For you created my inmost being; you knit me together in my mother's womb. I praise you because I am fearfully and wonderfully made." The female design is so incredible—and yet many women are ignorant of it.

Getting to Know Your Own Body

The sad fact is that while many mothers may have talked to their daughters about menstruation when they turned thirteen and about sex on the wedding night, very few ever described the details of a woman's anatomy.

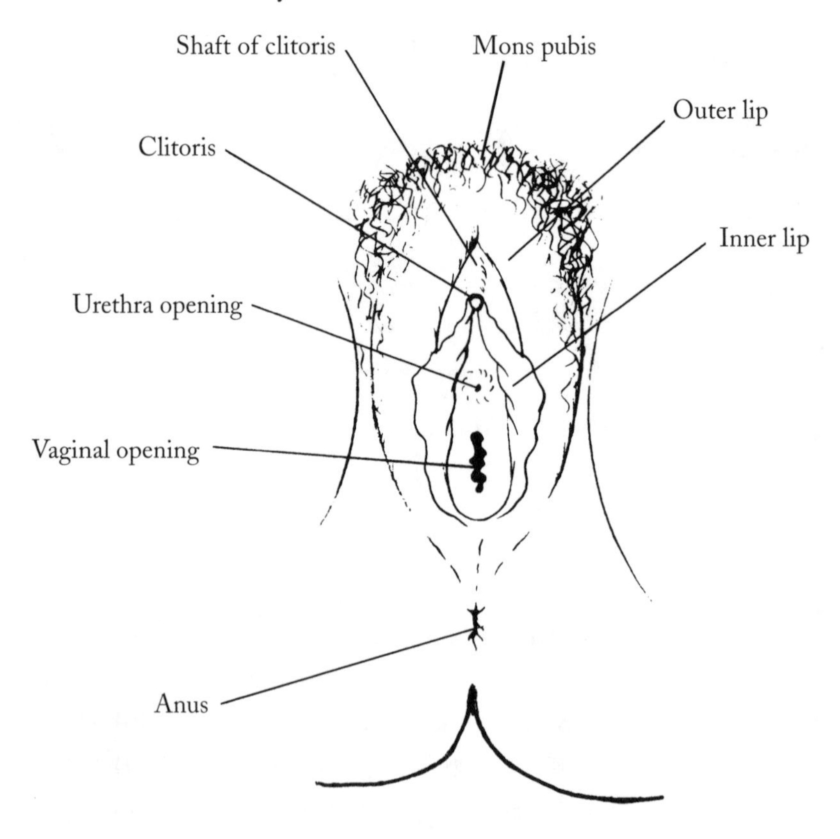

Picture of the external genitalia or the vulva[1]

If you are like most women, looking at your genitalia (from a Latin word that means to give birth) is not part of your usual routine. As children you were probably taught not to touch, look at, or talk about "down there" or your "privates." God placed your genitalia in a naturally hidden area, enveloped in soft folds of skin and tucked away between your thighs. So it isn't a surprise that women's genitalia have become a mystery, even to you and me.

When I tell a client to go home and examine herself with a hand mirror she'll usually say, "Oh no, it's disgusting or embarrassing or ugly." I've never had one woman come back and tell me she thought her genitalia were wonderful, beautiful, or amazing. And yet God exclaims of the creation he made, "It is very good." The female anatomy is exquisitely designed and is extraordinary in function. It has been likened in appearance to a flower.

A woman needs to know her physical body, and especially her genitalia, so that she will be aware if something is wrong or different from the usual. This includes knowing the correct names of the genitalia, their function, and how they work together.

Knowing her body also helps a woman discover how to obtain pleasure and greater sexual satisfaction. As a woman learns how to appreciate her anatomy, it will make it easier to accept and enjoy her God-given sexuality.

The External Sexual Anatomy

The mons or mons pubis is the fat layer that cushions the pubic bone and is covered with skin and pubic hair. The mons contains countless nerve endings and many women report stimulation of this area is very exciting.

The outer lips of the vulva or the labia majora are the folds of skin containing nerves and blood vessels that protect the opening to the vagina and urethra. These lips swell with blood when a woman is sexually excited.

The inner lips or labia minora are the smaller, hairless folds of skin inside the outer lips. They too engorge with blood and enlarge when a woman is sexually aroused. The labia come together over the head of the clitoris, forming the "hood" of the clitoris. This hood protects the delicate clitoris and has been likened to the foreskin of the penis. The labia minora ends just beneath the vagina.

I had a client I'll name Dottie. She came for counseling complaining of not being orgasmic. I realized after talking to her that she and her husband both thought her clitoris was inside the opening to the vagina. They had literally spent hours massaging the opening to her vagina, thrusting with his penis, even using a vibrator—all to no avail. When I drew a diagram to show her where her clitoris was and that it, not the vagina, was the ignition of her orgasm (so to speak), she almost cried with relief. I would estimate that nearly half of the people I see for sex therapy don't understand the exact location of the female genitalia in their relation to each other.

The clitoris looks like a tiny button of flesh and has an extremely dense network of blood vessels and nerves which makes it supersensitive. The sole purpose of the clitoris is pleasure, and it is the trigger of orgasm for most females. *It is the only organ in the female body made just to give us pleasure.*

The clitoris also engorges with blood during excitement and typically enlarges in diameter. The size of the clitoris varies from one woman to the next, and as with men, size has no impact on sexual pleasure. Sensitivity varies from woman to woman as well.

Some find much pleasure in prolonged stimulation of the clitoris, while others find direct touching can be uncomfortable.

While a woman is being aroused, a teasing type of touch to the clitoris can be very stimulating. Touching the clitoris then stroking the leg or breast, then back to the clitoris helps build anticipation and arousal. Men may be under the impression that what they like on their penis—firm direct stroking—is what arouses a woman. That is usually not the case, especially in the beginning phases of sexual arousal for the female.

The urethra is the opening to the bladder. It is only about one-half-inch long. Since the urethra is so short, bladder infections can result from bacteria being pushed into the bladder during intercourse. In a personal interview, urologist Dr. Paul Vasquez told me, "It's important to drink a glass of water before sex and then urinate after each lovemaking session, thus flushing out any unwanted bacteria and preventing a urinary infection."

Understanding the Vagina

Hannah and her husband, John, came to therapy assuming that Hannah was frigid. John assured me that he had tried everything to help Hannah have an orgasm but nothing worked. He actually thought that something was wrong with her vagina, even though her gynecologist had told both of them that she was completely normal.

When I asked what their lovemaking procedure was, John told me he would kiss her a little, put KY Jelly on his penis, and begin penetration. He said her vagina was too small for him and he could not enter her. Hannah hadn't said two words since they had entered my office, although I had directed every question to her. At that point I realized that I had a lot of teaching and training to do with this couple.

The vagina, from the Latin word for "sheath," is not just a mere sheath. It can expand and contract, is very powerful, changes with hormonal differences, lubricates, and even self-cleans. It is typically three to six inches long, about two to three inches wide, and collapses upon itself when not in an aroused state. Sizes and shapes of vaginas can vary, but most women's vaginas will accommodate to fit their husband's size and will not be a deterrent to sexual pleasure.[2]

The first layer of the vagina is warm and moist and contains glands which secrete a cleansing film of moisture. It lubricates itself even more during the excitement phase of lovemaking. The tissue lies in folds which allow it to expand and contract and grip the husband's penis during intercourse.

The second layer of the vagina is made of muscle and elastic tissue, again helping with contraction and expansion.

The third layer is made of fibrous tissue and a network of blood vessels that surround the vagina. When a woman is sexually excited, these blood vessels swell with blood and send lubricating fluid to the inside of the vagina.[3]

The first signal of arousal in a woman is when her vagina lubricates. This is just like a man getting an erection when he is aroused. At this time the vagina increases in length and width and even balloons out to accommodate the penis. At times the vagina can even make unusual sounds when it expels trapped air during intercourse.

Women sometimes wonder if their partner's penis is too big or too small for them. God has made the vagina an exceptionally accepting organ that can adjust to almost any size penis. Women who feel their husband's penis is too large may not be relaxed at the beginning of intercourse and tension can prevent the vagina from expanding. Women need to be very relaxed in order to enjoy the pleasures of intimacy. It may require taking a hot bath, taking more time in foreplay, or having her husband give her a back rub to help her get to that relaxed state.

Poor lubrication may also be a cause for feeling discomfort with a large penis. Once again, more foreplay gives the vagina a chance to begin lubricating and expanding. Using a water-based lubricant can also help. I've discovered that many couples aren't aware that it's important to lubricate the vagina and the penis.

Having the husband insert his penis very slowly, using a back and forth motion, is also a way to enhance lovemaking and decrease any initial discomfort. Another option is that the woman can choose a position that gives her the most control over the depth of penetration. This is usually the woman on top straddling the man. She then can use her thigh muscles to lift herself up and control the depth and rate of insertion.

If a woman feels her husband's penis is too small, strengthening the muscles around the vagina can help. Kegel exercises, named after the doctor who developed them, are a way of tightening the PC or pubococcygens muscles of the genitals. A woman can tell where these muscles are by beginning to urinate and then tightening up to stop the flow of urine. The muscles she has to contract to stop the flow of urine are the PC muscles. Many doctors also recommend these exercises to be done for stress incontinence of the bladder. Doing the contractions as many times a day as you can is best. Many doctors recommend doing ten contractions three times a day.[4] The PC muscles contract during orgasm, so practicing contracting them also can help a woman have a more enjoyable orgasm.

Experimenting with different positions is another way to increase your pleasure if your husband has a smaller penis. The position of the rear entry to the vagina while the woman is on hands and knees or on her side can give her more feeling as the penis will create friction from contacting the anterior wall of the vagina. If the woman is on the bottom she may need to pull her knees all the way up against her chest and place a pillow under her buttocks. Moving the hips from side to side, not just back and forth, can allow the penis to touch the vaginal walls increasing penile-vaginal friction.

The opening to the vagina and the lower one-third of the vagina tends to hold the most nerve endings and are thus the most sensitive areas. The upper two-thirds, near the cervix and uterus, do not have as many nerve endings as the lower third and are not as sensitive. This is significant since many men feel that having a longer penis would give their wives more pleasure. In truth, women experience the most sensitivity only within the first one or two inches of the vagina.

Some women have an area on the anterior wall, about two to three inches from the opening, which is called the G-spot, named after the German doctor who discovered it, Dr. Ernst Grafenberg. It is a bumpy area about the size of a dime and when stimulated it can arouse some women and bring them to orgasm.

Since the vagina is a self-cleaning organ, most doctors agree that douching is unnecessary unless ordered for a specific problem. Secretions of the vagina are normal, but if they are accompanied by itching or burning, have an unpleasant odor, or are a different color than normal, a woman should seek medical care. These symptoms can signal a bacterial infection, a yeast infection, a sexually transmitted disease, or an allergic reaction.

Hannah and her husband were given instruction about the female anatomy, particularly the vagina, and also the female sexual response cycle (which will be discussed in depth in the next chapter). Hannah found that she needed at least thirty minutes of foreplay in order to relax and begin to get aroused and lubricate.

Once she was lubricating, her vagina expanded and she was able to have intercourse with no problem.

But Hannah still was not orgasmic. It took some individual sessions with Hannah to help her focus on her repressed anger toward her husband and teach her how to assertively—directly but without hostility—tell him how she felt. She had been very angry about his blaming her for the entire problem and calling her frigid. She lovingly confronted him in one of our sessions. A tense silence enveloped the room. Then, amazingly, he became very receptive. After a few more months of counseling they reported that everything was working just fine.

The hymen is the fragile tissue that surrounds the vagina without completely covering it. The first time a woman has sexual intercourse it usually tears the hymen and some small bleeding may occur. But it's possible to rupture the hymen with athletic events and some women only have a small hymen to begin with. The lack of bleeding on the wedding night does not mean a woman was any less a virgin.

The anus is the opening to the rectum and the exit for bowel waste. The anus also has hundreds of nerves and can be quite sensitive. The anus is surrounded by two sphincters (rings of muscle) that hold the opening tightly closed until you are ready to evacuate waste.

The area between the vagina and the anus is called the perineum. This area has many nerve endings and can be sensitive to touch.

The Breasts as a Sexual Organ

The breasts are also considered an external sex organ. The greater part of a woman's breast is fat and the rest is glands and ducts. The glands produce milk that flows through the ducts and comes out the nipples to feed infants.

Many women find it very sexually stimulating to have their breasts touched, sucked, or massaged. Hundreds of nerves are in the nipple, and when a woman is sexually aroused the nipple becomes hard and erect and the breasts enlarge. Breast surgery to enlarge or reduce size can change the sensitivity to the breasts and nipples, so a woman should discuss this with her doctor before surgery. Once again, size has no effect on the sexual response of breasts. Occasionally, a woman's breasts may be tender to the touch due to hormonal changes, nursing a new baby, menopause, menstruation, inflammation, or infection. If the tenderness persists, a woman should always seek medical care.

Some women can even have an orgasm simply from breast stimulation. One couple had difficulty because the wife's nipples were so sensitive that she would have an orgasm too early in their lovemaking to suit either of them. They came to see me because they thought she was abnormal. I explained she had a low orgasmic threshold and was very fortunate to have an orgasm so easily. They rearranged their sexual agenda and did many other types of foreplay before nipple stimulation. Then, when they were ready for her to have an orgasm, her husband would begin nipple stimulation and she could easily have her orgasm.

The Internal Sexual Organs

The genitals in an unaroused or quiescent state are shown in the figure on page 69. This drawing, taken from *The New Sex Therapy* by Helen Singer Kaplan, shows where the organs lie in proximity to each other.[5]

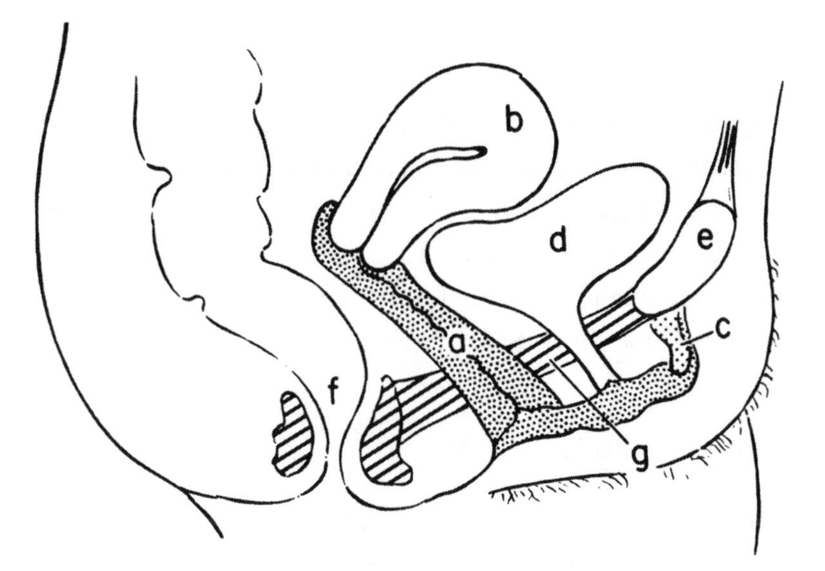

The internal female genitals: The vagina (a) is a dry, collapsed potential space. The uterus (b) is in its normal pelvic position. The clitoris (c) hangs ventrally. (d) represents the urinary bladder, while (e) is the pubic bone and (f) the anus. (g) is a schematic representation of the pubococcygens and bulbocavernosus muscles.

The cervix is the opening to the uterus and is at the very end of the vagina (a). It is the opening from the uterus into the vagina. A test called a Pap smear should be done yearly to be sure your cervix is healthy.

The uterus can be seen in the above drawing (b) and is normally the size of the fist. The uterus contracts during orgasm along with the lower vagina and pelvic floor muscles.

The fallopian tubes extend from the sides of the uterus. An egg takes one of these tubes as the pathway to the uterus. The fallopian tubes can become infected by a variety of sexually transmitted diseases. If this happens, sex may become very painful, and the infection needs to be treated by a physician.

The ovaries are the two almond-shaped organs that are at the end of each fallopian tube. They produce the female hormones estrogen, progesterone, and testosterone. They release the eggs that flow through the fallopian tubes and implant in your uterus.

Whether you've always understood the physiological aspects of your body or whether you are learning something new, I hope a better understanding of the female body leaves you amazed and grateful for God's intricate design.

Points to Consider

1. Since the vagina is a self-cleaning organ, douching should only be used when specifically recommended by your doctor for a certain problem.
2. After intercourse, a tampon can be placed in the vagina, temporarily, to absorb any semen. This prevents leakage of semen.
3. Chemicals can be absorbed through the walls of the vagina, so it's important to be very careful what you insert into the vagina.
4. Bacteria in stool can cause an infection if introduced into the vagina, so always wipe from front to back.
5. Be sure to wash your genitals after sex and before going to bed for the night. Rinsing away any residues of gels or lubricants helps to prevent irritation or infection. Also, drink a glass of water before sex and urinate after intercourse to prevent urinary infections.
6. Most doctors recommend avoiding feminine hygiene sprays since they can cause skin irritation, allergic reaction, and increase your possibility of getting a vaginal infection.

7. Wash the genitals daily with very mild or hypoallergenic soap. Be sure to wash between the labia and pull the hood of the clitoris back to wipe away any secretions that may reside between the hood and the clitoris. If these secretions are not removed they can cause pain with intercourse.
8. Lubricants should always be water based, not oil based like Vaseline. Oil-based lubricants can cause infection in the vagina and may weaken a condom or diaphragm.
9. If vaginal infections occur quite often, check what you may be using in the way of bubble bath, bath oil, or bath fragrances. Some products can cause vaginal infections.
10. Call your doctor or nurse practitioner if you notice any odor, unusual discharge, or itching and burning from the vagina. Infections can be caused by bacteria, yeast, or a parasite called *Trichomonas*.

The Stages of Lovemaking

A kiss is a lovely trick of nature to stop speech when words become unnecessary.

Ingrid Bergman

Morgan and Grant are a lovely young couple who came to see me because they felt their intimacy had deteriorated. They had been married for six months and had been happy sexually until the last two months. Lately, Morgan began having growing reluctance to having sexual relations with Grant. She said that before she was able to be intimate she had to have two things. First, Grant was to rub her back for thirty minutes. Second, he had to spend ten minutes assuring her that he loved her unconditionally and that he would never leave her. They came to see me because, even though Grant was meeting her conditions, she felt more and more disinterested in sex.

Our therapy began with *sensate focus* exercises. These are exercises that were designed by Masters and Johnson to help couples overcome performance anxiety and get in touch with their sensuous feelings. They consist of a series of massages.

I began their treatment instructing them to spend fifteen minutes at night giving each other a body massage without touching the genitals (to her relief and his horror). Grant was willing to go along with this as long as I reassured him it wouldn't last forever. After one week Morgan reported that she liked doing this and felt very comfortable with it.

Their next homework consisted of thirty minutes of massage adding in genital massage as well, but no orgasm or intercourse. Both were extremely aroused by this and Morgan felt this was evoking strong erotic sensations in her. I was pleased by their positive reaction to this assignment.

Due to her positive feedback, their next homework assignment was to give each other the massages, but after thirty minutes to continue on to intercourse if Morgan felt she was comfortable.

The following afternoon I received an alarming phone call. Morgan told me that as soon as they started to engage in intercourse after the massage she completely turned off sexually, felt anxious again, and stopped intercourse.

At this point I wanted to see Morgan alone. We talked about her seeming enjoyment of intimacy until intercourse started. She insisted that she was enjoying it, and then suddenly she felt anxious and just turned off. Upon exploration, it began to be apparent that she wasn't totally committed to this relationship and feared she had made a mistake in getting married.

As we plumbed the depths of her fears she realized she was afraid that her marriage would end in divorce as her parents' marriage had. We discussed her parents' problems. She felt her dad had been highly controlling and her mother had been extremely submissive. Her father had initiated the divorce with very little advance notice to her mother or Morgan. At the time Morgan was only six years old. Since the divorce she and her dad have not been close.

Because Morgan, unknowingly, feared abandonment by Grant, she always wanted to remain in control and be alert. She feared being blindsided like her mom had been. Morgan reasoned that if she gave in to her natural sexual response, Grant would gain a certain amount of control over her. As we discussed the situation, Morgan recognized that being out of control evoked anxiety. Her anxiety was the fear that Grant would eventually leave her. It was as if Morgan were a dog owner who thought the dog would run away if it wasn't held tightly on the leash. Morgan could never relax and let the normal sexual response take place. She felt Grant might leave if she wasn't continually on alert.

With this insight, she slowly began to recognize that she and Grant had none of the problems her parents had. They were both very much partners in their marriage and she began taking steps to work on her anxiety. Grant was patient and supportive, learning to reassure her of his devotion and consistency. They also spent time every day talking and connecting emotionally. Once she recognized this mistaken belief—a lack of sexual response would protect her from abandonment—she was able to allow her body to follow its natural sexual response. They were both Christian believers, had taken time to allow their relationship to grow and develop, and had all the attributes required for a good Christian marriage.

God is orderly and he created the orderly laws of nature (Gen. 8:22; 1 Cor. 14:40). One of those laws is the sexual response stages—with only some minor variations—through which all females go during lovemaking. Masters and Johnson first identified these stages as *excitement, plateau, orgasm,* and *resolution* (or the resting stage).[1]

Desire Develops into Excitement

While desire is not included as one of these stages, it does precede and even begins the development of excitement. Desire encompasses thinking about or having the physical or emotional feeling of being willing to participate in sex or to seek it out. Desire ebbs and flows and is influenced by internal factors such as hormones, health, and external factors like the closeness of the relationship and if the kids are asleep. It is ignited differently in different women.

Sometimes a woman's sexual tension builds and she feels a physical desire for sex. Many times a woman feels this tension right before her menstrual period starts or immediately after it's over. However, some women don't ever feel their sexual tension in a physical sense. For them, sex is more of a thought that they would like to participate in sex.

Many women need an emotional connection in the relationship—to feel loved and bonded—before their desire is ignited. I try to help men see that women are like fires—they go out if unattended. For some women their desire is expressed as the decision to engage in the sexual cycle because they know that they won't get that "turned on" feeling until ten to thirty minutes after sex has begun.

Feeling loved and connected is differently defined by each individual woman. In marriage seminars, I ask women what makes them desire sex. Sometimes it's the sweet way the husband plays with the kids. Or the husband folds the laundry without her asking. Or they talk and share things about their day. Or simply, the physical desire that she feels. The woman's answers usually demonstrate what the woman perceives as love and consideration. *It's the small things that build the inward desire in women.*

> I try to help men see that women are like fires—they go out if unattended.

Because our thoughts are part of the driving force of our desire, what we focus on is what develops. When a woman focuses on sex by thinking about a wonderful time she and her husband had making love, it stimulates desire and develops into more enjoyable lovemaking.

According to one woman I counseled, she never thought about sex. I had her write down in her weekly calendar a time each Tuesday and Friday when she would visualize a wonderful lovemaking session she'd had early in her marriage. The more she began to focus on their special sexual intimacy, and how much she enjoyed it when she took the time, the more interested she was in having sex. Proverbs 23:7 says, "As he thinks within himself, so he is." That goes for a woman, too. What she focused on is what developed!

Sexual Response Stage #1—Excitement

The first stage of the sexual response cycle is called the excitement phase. This usually happens after foreplay has already begun since the female needs and enjoys the touching, kissing, and stimulation to become aroused. This phase begins when definite physical changes occur:

1. Vaginal lubrication begins and a woman feels wet.
2. Nipples become erect.
3. Blood flow increases the size of labia and clitoris.
4. Blood pressure, heart rate and respirations increase.
5. The uterus moves up in the pelvis, lengthening the vagina.
6. The breasts enlarge.
7. Sex flush occurs in 50 to 75 percent of women.

The sex flush is a spotty reddish skin color change that occurs over the breasts and abdomen. It comes from a change in the pattern of blood flow.[2]

If I had to identify one problem for which I counsel couples the most, it's this: ***Not allowing enough time in foreplay for the female to become truly aroused and enter into the excitement phase.***

Most women whom I have seen require at least fifteen to forty minutes of foreplay before they are fully aroused. When a woman is rushed, she is less likely to have an orgasm. It is a wise man who holds back and waits for his wife to be as aroused as he is.

There is a direct correlation between how long a couple spends in foreplay and how frequently a woman has an orgasm. There is also a direct correlation between how frequently a woman reaches orgasm and how sexually satisfied she reports that she is. It's only logical that if a woman has ample foreplay she has a better chance of having an orgasm, and if she has an orgasm she will report more sexual satisfaction.

At our seminars we always teach "ladies first," meaning a woman needs to have her orgasm first. Once a man ejaculates, it's hard for him to stay in a sexual mood and have the energy to bring his wife to orgasm. So "ladies first" becomes part of a healthy sexual life. A woman will want to have sex again much sooner if she, too, has had an orgasm.

Some women tell me, "I don't have to have an orgasm every time, I just like feeling close." Sometimes that's true, but other times a woman has confessed to me that she says this because she is afraid that her husband is getting tired of how much foreplay she needs for an orgasm. She doesn't want him to get irritated or angry, so she says, "You go ahead and come, and we won't worry about me this time." Then she's left with frustration due to the buildup of unreleased sexual tension. Over time, this can grow into anger and resentment and the wife becomes disinterested in sex altogether.

Sexual Response Stage #2—Plateau

As excitement builds, the vagina tightens at the outside end and widens and balloons at the end near the cervix. This is called the orgasmic platform. This allows the penis to be gripped tighter at the outer end of the vagina causing greater enjoyment for the man. It also allows the sperm to pool at the cervix and travel into the uterus. The uterus becomes more elevated. The blood pressure, pulse, and respirations continue to increase and there is more blood flow to the genitals. In this stage the clitoris seems to pull back under the hood, but it is still engorged with blood. The inner lips enlarge dramatically pushing the outer lips apart. Once this happens, vivid color changes occur in the inner lips changing from pink to bright red or a deeper wine color.[3]

There is an ebb and flow to the excitement during this plateau stage. Most women feel this phase is enjoyable and their excitement continues to build during this time. However, some women may feel like they were cooking with gas and someone suddenly cut the pipe and extinguished the fire. Or they may feel as if they had their foot on the accelerator, but suddenly ran out of gas. They keep pushing the accelerator but the car has stalled.

Here is a sample of what many women tell me they think during the plateau:

"I bet he's getting tired; I better hurry up and let him come."
"I'm not feeling that excitement anymore so I'll mentally plan dinner."
"Why does this always happen to me? I almost reach orgasm and then it just stops! I must be defective."
"Sex is so easy for my husband; why can't it be that easy for me?"

The plateau stage sabotages many women because, if the excitement wanes, they think the party is over. They assume they won't have an orgasm so they let go of the sexual mind-set. Since a great deal of sex is in the mind, it's important to discipline the mind to concentrate on the good feelings and not drift to other thoughts. A woman may have never known that letting her mind drift to other things could be impeding her intimacy with her husband, but it is true.

Instead of giving up during the plateau, a woman can do three things to reignite the flame:

1. *Be optimistic.* Instead of thinking, "I was excited and then it just went away. I guess I won't be having an orgasm tonight," recognize that this is the plateau stage and there are ways to get going again.
2. *Be focused.* Keep the mind focused on the sensuality of sex, the pleasurable feelings of stroking, kissing, etc. Use the

imagery of wonderful times of lovemaking that have resulted in orgasm in the past.

3. *Be persevering.* Continue stimulating the clitoris because the arousal will return.

God wants us to keep our sex life healthy. Sometimes it takes disciplining our thoughts to enhance our intimacy with our mates. During lovemaking, a woman's thoughts often turn to fantasy. Fantasy is defined as an imagined event or sequence of mental images, such as a daydream. Most fantasies of the women I've counseled play out like a romance novel: *My husband wants me but I have to say no. He chases me around the desk, catches me, tells me I'm so beautiful, and starts kissing me. I try to resist but he convinces me and I give in.*

These fantasies involve different settings, styles, places, or atmospheres that help keep their love life novel and exciting, but usually are not detrimental to the marriage in any way. If a woman so desires, she can share her fantasies with her husband and even play them out at times. I've had clients who purchased nurse caps, waitress aprons, and even a superwoman cape that turned their lovemaking into fireworks just by being creative.

Of course, fantasies can be unhealthy and perverted if they involve anyone but your husband, are harmful or demeaning, or include anyone else besides the couple.

Sexual Response Stage #3—Orgasm

Orgasm is a whole body response, not just something that happens in the genitals. Muscles in many different areas of the body contract and brain wave patterns change. Orgasm is when the body suddenly discharges its accumulated sexual tension in a peak of sexual arousal.

Orgasm can be called a "climax" or "coming," but whatever you call it, it's still an orgasm. Again, several bodily changes occur.

1. Rhythmic contractions in the vagina, uterus, pelvic floor muscles, and rectal sphincter occurring at 0.8-second intervals
2. Peak distribution of the sex flush
3. Frequently, strong muscle contractions in other body parts
4. Increased blood pressure, pulse, and respiration
5. Vocalizations or holding one's breath[4]

Comparable to the penis, the clitoris has a dense network of blood vessels and nerves which make it supersensitive and the trigger for orgasm for the majority of women. Some women can come to orgasm with just vaginal thrusting, but for the preponderance of women, asking them to have an orgasm with vaginal thrusting *only* and no clitoral stimulation is like asking a man to have an orgasm with only his scrotum being stroked. It would be difficult, indeed.

Many people have debated the vaginal versus clitoral argument, but any orgasm is right and good, and it doesn't matter where the woman perceives it began. Wherever she discerns the stimulation to occur—vagina or clitoris—an orgasm is still breathtaking and is a physical release of built-up sexual tension.

Just as a woman can't "will" herself to deliver her baby when she wants to, she can't "will" herself to have an orgasm. Both are naturally occurring phenomena that happen as a reflexive response. In both processes, however, relaxation helps. A woman who is relaxed can allow her body to do what it already knows how to do—have an orgasm. Relaxation involves staying in the moment, mentally, physically, and emotionally. Anxiety and orgasm never mix.

One client stated, "My husband could have sex in an earthquake, but I need to be relaxed, calm, have the kids in bed, and not be too tired to reach orgasm. Why is that?" Typically, an orgasm is more difficult for women to attain than most men. An orgasm is a fragile thing for a woman and many times the atmosphere has to be *right.* What "right" means for each woman is different.

"When can't you have an orgasm?" Here are some answers.

1. "When I think the kids can hear us."
2. "When I feel fat, out of shape, or ugly."
3. "When I'm angry, because this is the first time my husband has spent any length of time with me today."
4. "When I am too tired and it's late at night before he mentions he'd like to have sex."
5. "When I'm not feeling emotionally close to him."
6. "When we're in a rush and I have to hurry."
7. "When I don't feel physically well."
8. "When I'm really worried about something."
9. "When my husband's hygiene is poor or I find him unappealing."
10. "When I feel like he is pressuring me to have an orgasm."
11. "When he wants to try a position or technique I don't like."

Some women have never experienced an orgasm (this will be discussed at length in chapter nine). One client, when asked if she was orgasmic, stated, "Tell me what it feels like, and I'll tell you if I ever had one."

Most couples have consecutive orgasms, first one person then the other. This way the wife can focus totally on her own orgasm and then help her husband reach his, or vice versa.

I'm always asked about simultaneous orgasms. They are difficult to attain and many clients report that, if and when they happen, they aren't as wonderful as they had expected. A famous sex therapist and psychologist at the University of Utah, D. Cory Hammond, said of simultaneous orgasms, "Ask your clients what other bodily functions they do simultaneously."

Sometimes a woman feels as if an orgasm is explosive like fireworks, and some women see special colors with different orgasms, they have told me. Some describe a moment of suspended animation, dissociation, or a sense of being out of this world. Most feel some type of intensely pleasurable feelings that spread throughout their body along with the pelvic contractions. Sometimes orgasms are milder and much less intense, but the satisfaction can be just as good with an intense orgasm as a mild one. Since an orgasm is so subjective, it's how the woman interprets the orgasm that determines how satisfied she is.

Many variables determine what the orgasm may be like that day, including hormone levels, time since last orgasm, illness, fatigue, emotional connection to partner, time pressure, and so forth.

Some women can have multiple orgasms and some can only have one at a time. But again, it isn't always the intensity or the length of the orgasm that makes it great to that particular woman; it's how she interprets it.

Sexual Stage #4: Resolution

At the resolution stage the woman returns to the unaroused state. All the changes that occurred in the three preceding stages reverse as the body returns to its resting state.

The sex flush disappears, the color changes of the labia disappear, the uterus moves back to its former place, the orgasmic platform disappears, and the vagina returns to normal size. Blood pressure, pulse, and respirations all decrease, and the muscles of the entire body relax. Stimulation of the genitals at this time may be uncomfortable or irritating to some women.

If a woman has been aroused but has not come to orgasm, there may be a slower return to normal. The blood congestion takes longer to subside and the female may feel a genital heaviness or throbbing. Sometimes women can experience an orgasm in their sleep or wake up having an orgasm as the body discharges the sexual tension.[5]

A woman's resolution has been likened to a parachute slowly coming down, while a man's resolution has been likened to a dive-bomber. Women slowly float down from the pink cloud but men seem to drop to the sandman fairly quickly. Women usually enjoy the holding and closeness of the afterglow and particularly some communication of love and affection.

Healthy partners will compromise on the amount of time spent on the afterglow since a woman might like it to be longer and her husband might prefer it to be shorter.

Sex as God's Gift to Women

Until the mid-twentieth century, sex was seen predominantly as something the man did to the woman for his pleasure alone. Women were taught to do their duty and have sex with their husbands, but proper women were not supposed to like it.

A pamphlet entitled, *Instruction and Advice for the Young Bride* by Ruth Smythers, wife of Reverend Smythers, pastor of the Arcadian Methodist Church, was written in 1894. It begins by saying:

> To the sensitive young woman who has had the benefits of proper upbringing, the wedding day is the happiest and the most terrifying of her life. . . . On the negative side, there is the wedding night, during which the bride must pay the piper, so to speak, by facing the TERRIBLE experience of sex. . . . One

cardinal rule of marriage should never be forgotten: GIVE LITTLE, GIVE SELDOM, AND ABOVE ALL GIVE GRUDGINGLY!

Thankfully, God has liberated us from those dark ages and brought us into the light of his gift of love and intimacy.

Points to Consider

1. The four stages are excitement, plateau, orgasm, and resolution or the resting stage.
2. Desire is the thought or physical or emotional feeling of being willing to participate in sex or to seek it out.
3. What we focus on is what develops. Women can focus on sex with their husbands by thinking about it more, so it can develop into enjoyable lovemaking.
4. Typically, women need twenty to thirty minutes of foreplay to be completely aroused.
5. By being optimistic, focused, and persevering a woman can traverse the plateau stage.
6. Orgasms vary from woman to woman and can be clitoral, vaginal, singular, or multiple.
7. Since orgasm is so subjective, it's how the woman interprets the orgasm that determines how satisfied she is.
8. Many variables determine what an orgasm may be like that day, including hormone level, time since last orgasm, illness, fatigue, emotional connection to partner, time pressure, and so forth.
9. The resolution stage is when the genitalia return to the resting state.
10. Healthy partners will compromise on how much time to spend in afterglow since most women would like more time and most men would like less.

Sexuality and Hormones

To everything there is a season and
a time for every purpose under heaven.

ECCLESIASTES 3:1

Hormones! Just the word conjures up dread in women. We aren't exactly sure which hormones are accountable for what responses, but we do know that they wreak havoc with our lives at times. However, hormones also play a vital role in our sexuality. It's important that we understand how they do this.

The Role of Estrogen

Produced by the ovaries, adrenal glands, and in the fatty tissues, estrogen is one of the most significant hormones for females. Various systems throughout a woman's body have receptor sites for estrogen: the reproductive system, urinary system, digestive system, skin, bones, and even the brain. The body produces three different types of estrogen:

estradiol—the most powerful estrogen, produced by the ovaries,
estrone—made in the body's fatty tissues
estriol—a weaker estrogen most abundant during pregnancy.

Estrogen has a number of functions in the body. It's responsible for the secondary sexual characteristics such as breast and genital development. It helps produce collagen (the connective tissue that keeps skin supple and elastic), maintains the moisture and elasticity of the vagina, helps maintain the strength of the bladder tissues, helps memory and mood, and even protects our bones and gums. But one of the major jobs of estrogen is to build up the lining of the uterus in preparation to receive a fertilized egg.[1]

Three times in a woman's life her estrogen levels drop:

1. Just prior to menstrual flow estrogen levels decline rapidly. Thirty-five percent of women have moderate premenstrual syndrome symptoms of irritability, mood fluctuations, and fatigue. Three percent suffer severe symptoms.
2. Just after childbirth estrogen levels plummet and can be one hundred times less than during pregnancy.

3. From age twenty until menopause estrogen levels begin to decline. When menstruation ceases, estrogen levels have fallen by 75 to 80 percent. This may affect a woman's mood, memory, and sexuality.[2]

Wendy was an energetic, beautiful woman of fifty who came to see me after intercourse with her husband became painful. She said she had easily breezed through menopause with very few symptoms, five years prior to seeing me. She had been adamant about not taking hormone replacement therapy since, as she put it, "her mother had never taken estrogen and she was eighty-nine years old and doing well." Wendy was trim, ate healthfully, exercised daily, and worked full-time. The pain during intercourse had begun two years prior, but she had been too embarrassed to seek help until coming to see me.

After taking a detailed history it appeared that Wendy and her husband had an excellent relationship in every way, with the exception of painful intercourse (also known as dyspareunia). When I asked her why she hadn't talked to her gynecologist about this, she said she just assumed that because she was so healthy, it must be a psychological problem.

I explained to Wendy what estrogen did for the body and how a woman's estrogen production drops throughout her lifetime. I stressed how most menopausal women had some need for vaginal estrogen to nourish and moisturize the vagina. I clarified that vaginal estrogen only works locally on the tissues of the vagina, not systemically throughout her whole body. This allayed her fears since she was resistant to taking estrogen for fear of weight gain.

I sent Wendy to her gynecologist and requested she ask for vaginal estrogen suppositories, cream, or an estrogen ring that can be inserted into the vagina. I also advised her to talk to her gynecologist about the other pros and cons of hormone replacement therapy (HRT) and to keep an open mind.

She called me a month later to report that she had begun the vaginal estrogen, her pain was gone, and she was enjoying her sexuality once again. Her doctor had also checked her bone density and had put her on a preparation called Actonel to help with thinning bones since she was not willing to consider HRT.

The Role of Progesterone

Progesterone is another hormone that is also produced in the ovaries. Progesterone protects us from experiencing too much estrogen before menopause. It also prepares the lining of the uterus for implanting the fertilized egg and maintains pregnancy by sustaining that lining. Progestins are a synthetic form of progesterone. There is really no good data relating progestins to changes in a woman's sexual desire.[3]

The Role of Testosterone

Many women think that testosterone is just for men, but not so. Testosterone is a hormone that is also essential to female sexuality. Just as men's bodies manufacture testosterone, so do women's bodies. Testosterone is produced through the ovaries and adrenal glands.

Testosterone has many talents. It can improve libido and energy, strengthen bones, improve cognitive functioning, and promote a sense of well-being; it helps maintain muscle mass, nipple, and clitoris sensitivity to pleasure.

Just as the production of estrogen slows down with age, so does the body's production of testosterone. By age forty, women produce only about 50 percent of the testosterone they did at age twenty.[4] The levels drop even further with menopause or a hysterectomy and surgical removal of the ovaries.

While women need estrogen for moisture and nourishment of the vagina, we also need testosterone in order to feel desire and experience a biological sexual response. In her book, *The Hormone of Desire,* Dr. Susan Rako outlines the most obvious signs of testosterone deficiency:

1. Overall decreased sexual desire
2. Diminished vital energy and sense of well-being
3. Decreased sensitivity to sexual stimulation in the clitoris and nipples
4. Overall decreased arousability and capacity for orgasm
5. Thinning and loss of pubic hair[5]

S-E-X and P-M-S: Sexuality and Premenstrual Syndrome

Each month after ovulation, estrogen and progesterone levels change. For some women, this change brings on symptoms of tension, irritability, emotional ups and downs, bloating, breast tenderness, sadness, headaches, and food cravings. A woman can experience PMS anytime after menstruation first begins at puberty and can vary in severity throughout a woman's life. Symptoms of PMS usually begin two to ten days before menstruation occurs. If the symptoms become severe they meet the criteria for a disorder called Premenstrual Dysphoric Disorder that may be treated with antidepressants.

Some women don't want anything to do with sex during their premenstrual part of the month, some can take sex or leave it, and some feel as if they have the most sexual desire during that time. This is definitely one way in which we know that no two women are alike. Sexual reactions to the premenstrual time of month differ widely from woman to woman.

Sexuality during Pregnancy

While estrogen and progesterone are produced in major amounts during pregnancy, a woman's desire for sexuality during pregnancy can increase, decrease, or remain the same. Typically, sexual activity declines in the last two months of pregnancy. Studies prove that, overall, if a woman feels happy about the pregnancy and believes she is attractive even though pregnant, she will report adequate sexual satisfaction.[6]

Pregnancy is also a good time to try different positions that may accommodate a woman's enlarged proportions. Instead of just seeing the change in her body as interfering with her sexual relationships, this can be a time for discovering other enjoyable aspects of lovemaking.

Sexuality after Childbirth

An episiotomy is a surgical incision that runs from the vagina down into the perineum. Episiotomies are performed during childbirth to facilitate the birth and prevent tearing of the perineum. Note that 62 to 90 percent of women who have vaginal births have episiotomies.[7]

It usually takes three to six weeks for the stitches to heal and for the area to become pain free. Even after the initial healing from the episiotomy has begun, just the thought of sex can be painful for a while. Sexual positions such as the female on top position or "spoons" position may be preferable because they allow the woman to control the depth of penile penetration. And because the hormonal drop after birth is great, the vagina may be dry and some type of lubrication should be used.

It's estimated that between 50 to 70 percent of women experience baby blues or postpartum depression in the first seven to ten days after childbirth.[8] This brief episode can entail some tearfulness but usually passes quickly. However, serious postpartum depression can occur from one week to one year after the birth. Symptoms can include changes in appetite and sleeping patterns, crying daily, and loss of interest in usual activities. Unusual feelings of anger and hopelessness and thoughts of death or suicide may also be part of postpartum depression. This type of severe depression is almost always treated with antidepressants and therapy. A woman's sex drive is usually nonexistent if she is suffering from this type of depression.

Sexuality after a Cesarean Section Surgery

If a woman has had a Cesarean section in order to deliver her baby, she has gone through major surgery and may need a good four to six weeks for the muscles and uterus to heal. Although there is no surgery to the vagina, time is still needed to recover from the abdominal surgery, much less get used to the energy required to take care of the infant.

Sexual positions that are best after a C-section are ones which put no pressure directly on top of the female since the incision sight may be sensitive. Positions like the spoons position or facing each other side to side can be used. Many times sexual relations are put off until the woman feels recovered and has the strength to take care of the baby and herself.

Sexuality and Breast-Feeding

Prolactin is a hormone secreted by the pituitary gland that stimulates milk production and also inhibits ovulation. Nursing mothers have high levels of prolactin, which is why breast-feeding usually stops a woman from experiencing her monthly menstrual time. However, some women do still ovulate while breast-feeding, so it is vital to use birth control if another pregnancy is not planned at that time.

Prolactin also lowers estrogen production and decreases libido. Many breast-feeding mothers are not aware of these hormonal changes and may wonder why they have little sex drive. Breast-feeding couples should be aware that during orgasm milk may erupt from the nipples due to the release of oxytocin. Nursing the baby prior to lovemaking can reduce the likelihood of this happening.[9]

Sexuality during Perimenopause

Perimenopause actually means "around menopause." It typically begins sometime in a woman's forties but can happen in her thirties or fifties. Fluctuating progesterone levels in the perimenopausal years can result in unpredictable menstruation before it stops altogether. As estrogen production slows, the ovaries stop releasing eggs. A woman can begin to have some menopausal symptoms such as increased fatigue, loss of interest in sex, mood swings, insomnia, and hot flashes. As the ovaries slow down the

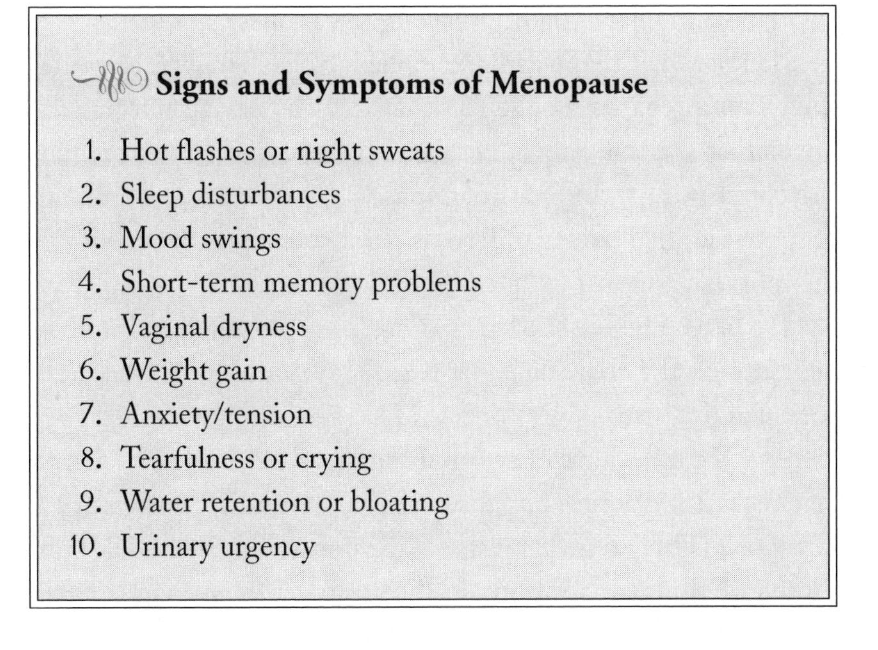

Signs and Symptoms of Menopause

1. Hot flashes or night sweats
2. Sleep disturbances
3. Mood swings
4. Short-term memory problems
5. Vaginal dryness
6. Weight gain
7. Anxiety/tension
8. Tearfulness or crying
9. Water retention or bloating
10. Urinary urgency

production of eggs and estrogen, the adrenal glands slow their hormone production of testosterone by 50 percent. Sexual desire can cool for approximately one-third of women.[10]

Sara came to see me with feelings of sadness that she thought were part of postpartum depression. Sara was thirty-five years old; she had had her first child at age thirty-three. She was pregnant with her second child when she had a miscarriage a few months prior to seeing me. She complained of feeling irritable and intensely sad, crying most days off and on. She had insomnia, poor concentration, and had lost her appetite. Her husband was concerned since she had also lost total interest in sex since the miscarriage.

While we were talking, Sara had a full-blown hot flash and we stopped while I got her some ice water. She certainly had symptoms of depression, but the hot flash was a red flag to me.

"How long have you been having hot flashes?" I asked.

"Is that what that was?" she replied. Since Sara was so young she was unprepared for the fact that she was having hot flashes. Given that she was only in her midthirties, Sara had no idea that she could be entering perimenopause. Sara went on to tell me that she had had irregular periods since the miscarriage, but she thought that was just to be expected.

We prayed before she left that day. I asked God to strengthen her through the challenges she faced and to not let her be incapacitated by them.

As a second course of action, I sent Sara to her obstetrician to be checked for perimenopause. She had a Follicle Stimulating Hormone (FSH) test that tests for the onset of menopause. If the results of this test are high, it shows that the woman is perimenopausal or menopausal. Sara's test was high; she had entered early menopause after the miscarriage. She and her doctor decided upon hormone replacement therapy and an antidepressant regimen. Within three months Sara was feeling much better.

Because she would most likely spend half of her life postmenopause, Sara made herself aware of the changes and perils she might face. She began taking calcium to prevent osteoporosis, stopped smoking, and started exercising. She became very careful about taking care of herself for the sake of her husband, her baby, and herself. Her mood became positive, and her interest in sexuality returned.

Sexuality during Menopause

Menopause with erratic periods usually comes on gradually. These erratic periods may happen for a number of months. When a full twelve months has gone by without a period, a woman typically is considered "through the change." However, it's important to remember that during the last stages of menopause a woman is still fertile and still can become pregnant.

Various studies show a loss of libido during menopause, some say as high as 40 percent of women.[11] Women who have reduced estrogen can have thinning and fragile vaginal tissues, shortened or narrowed vaginas, and possibly much less lubrication upon arousal. This can cause painful intercourse.

But it's the drop in testosterone levels that reduces a woman's desire for sex, affects her arousal capacity, and makes having an orgasm more difficult. Many women complain of feeling like they are numb below the waist and no longer have any desire for sex. They may have to struggle for a long time to have an orgasm and then find that it's much weaker than it was before. "Almost not worth the effort," reported one client.

Women differ to a great degree in their response to menopause. Some may be completely unaffected hormonally, while others are affected to varying degrees. However, menopause does affect these areas of your body in these specific ways:

Uterus—The blood supply to the uterus decreases as does the size and weight of the uterus.

Ovaries—Estrogen production and ovulation decrease and the ovaries shrink.

Vagina—The tissues become thinner and less elastic, and thus, more easily traumatized or damaged. The vagina narrows and shortens and can lose its muscle tone. Dyspareunia, pain upon intercourse, can occur. Infections may be more likely.

Urethra and bladder—Stress and urgency incontinence may occur. Discomfort upon urination may be present. More frequent urination may occur.

Breasts—Size may decrease, and there may be less firmness and more sagging.
Skin—May lose elasticity and be less firm.
Bones—Can lose density and become more thin and porous. There may be more possibility of fractures from osteoporosis.
Brain—More emotional fluctuation may be noticeable, along with slower thinking and some memory loss.

Women need to be frank and specific with their doctors and tell them of their exact symptoms so the doctor will know what to prescribe. At times the doctor may need to do blood chemistries to determine the levels of estrogen or testosterone. At other times, a woman won't need blood tests to confirm the obvious. But a woman needs to be aware of the possibilities and problems for treatment so that she can be an informed consumer and communicate with her doctor in an intelligent way.

Elaine and her husband came to see me as a last resort. Ed was very frustrated and Elaine was anxious. They'd been married twenty-nine years and had had a good sex life up until the past five years. Elaine had gone through menopause with very little problems. She had decided she did not want to take hormone replacement therapy since her mother had died of breast cancer and some studies show HRT can increase the risk of breast cancer. Within the previous six months Elaine reported that she had had absolutely no desire for sex and she felt as if she'd lost her capacity to have an orgasm. She stated that, along with her lack of desire and problems with orgasm, she also felt pain at the time of intercourse.

I suspected that Elaine was exhibiting signs of low estrogen and low testosterone. But with her history of family breast cancer,

I was unsure whether or not her doctor would prescribe vaginal estrogen cream. I called her medical doctor and spoke to him about Elaine. After examining Elaine, he ordered testosterone gel to be used nightly by applying it to the upper thigh or vulva.

Elaine also had signs of severe vaginal dryness. Again taking her family history of cancer into account, her doctor also ordered an over-the-counter moisturizing suppository called Replens® to be used three times a week. Since the testosterone was to be used locally in such a small dose, the occurrence of any masculine-type changes such as hair growth or lowered voice was minute.

Another preparation called Joy Gel™ was ordered and this was to be placed directly on her clitoris. I phoned Scott Snyder, pharmacist and owner of Custom Meds, a compounding pharmacy that made Joy Gel™. He explained that Joy Gel™ contained Viagra®, Isosorbide, and Arginine, all substances used to increase blood supply to the clitoris.

After using these preparations for a few months, the pain was eradicated and Elaine reported an increased feeling of desire for intimacy. It was still taking about forty minutes of foreplay for her to have an orgasm, but the time was decreasing with each encounter.

Testosterone and Estrogen Preparations

A testosterone pill combined with estrogen, called Estratest, is available. It contains methyltestosterone and estrogen, but it must be prescribed by a doctor. Even though testosterone has been available for years, no preparation of plain testosterone—a natural substance which cannot be patented—is marketed by any drug company for women. There is a testosterone gel for men called AndroGel, but the concentration is too high for women to use.

Testosterone also comes in different forms by itself, such as in gels, tablets, capsules, or small lozenges you can place under your tongue. All of these preparations must be originated by a compounding pharmacy since formulations small enough for women to use are not made by the large pharmaceutical companies. A compounding pharmacy is one that can take the testosterone and create the cream, gel, or lozenge. This also requires a prescription from your doctor. You can call the International Association of Compounding Pharmacies at 1-800-927-4227 to fill your doctor's prescription. Or you can contact Scott Snyder at Custom Meds at 1-800-226-2023. This company is able to ship meds anywhere in the United States.

Estrogen can come in pills, patches, creams, and a vaginal ring. It also must be prescribed by your doctor. Since there are a number of confusing combinations of hormones on the market, you need to communicate at length with your health care provider to see which, if any, is right for you. Certain risks sometimes preclude a woman from using HRT such as having a personal or family history of stroke, breast or uterine cancer, heart disease, blood clots, liver disease, heavy cigarette smoking, or high cholesterol levels. However, even with these risks a woman should talk to her doctor or nurse practitioner before deciding for or against HRT.

Hormone Replacement Therapy (HRT)

You may be one of the fortunate few who don't experience any of the common signs of menopause. But even if you do not have hot flashes, vaginal dryness, or other symptoms, your risks for heart disease, osteoporosis, and other menopause-related health problems may still increase just because you are menopausal.

Everywoman: The Essential Guide for Healthy Living states, "Whether to use hormone replacement therapy (HRT) is one of the most difficult choices to make. Estrogen can be prescribed alone, with progesterone, or with testosterone. Estrogen is one of the best strategies for relieving menopausal symptoms but there is no one size fits all medication for menopause."[12]

Hormone replacement therapy is prescribed as a short-term treatment for relief from menopausal symptoms like hot flashes and vaginal dryness. HRT may reduce the risk of osteoporosis, hip fracture, and colon cancer. But these potential benefits are often outweighed for women who have not had a hysterectomy by the increased risk of breast cancer, coronary heart disease, stroke, or blood clots as identified recently in the HRT portion of the Women's Health Initiative Study.

According to the National Institutes of Health, "Women with intact uteruses who are currently taking the combination therapy of estrogen and progestin for the relief of menopause symptoms may face an increased risk of breast cancer, coronary heart disease, stroke, and pulmonary embolism. After 5.2 years of follow-up in a multi-center clinical trial, results indicated that the combination therapy should not be initiated or continued for primary prevention of coronary heart disease. Those potentially affected should ask their doctor or nurse practitioners for more information and if this combination HRT should be continued."[13]

You can read more about these studies at http://www.nhlbi.nih.gov/health/women/q_a.htm>.

However, other experts in the field feel the hormone replacement trial by the National Institutes of Health may not have been correctly explained. In the Web MD Medical News for October 24, 2002, Michael Smith, MD, stated:

> The hormone replacement trial halted in July 2002 by the National Institutes of Health . . . may have been overstated. The original reports may have exaggerated the risks. The absolute risks are actually quite small. For example, the study projects that in 10,000 women, thirty-eight would get invasive breast cancer when taking hormones, while thirty would get it if they were *not* taking HRT. As a treatment for the symptoms of menopause, HRT is unmatched, and some women will undoubtedly choose to continue taking the therapy in spite of the risks. The study only applied to "Prempro," a mixture of estrogen and a progestin. However, there are other forms of HRT that are approved for treating menopause.[14]

As you can see, even the experts don't always agree on what should and should not be recommended. That's why it's vital to know your own body, know your risks, and talk with a doctor whom you trust to give you the very best information for your situation.

One panic-stricken client came to see me over the results of the National Institutes of Health study. She had decided to just take herself off of her HRT—which she should never have done without first consulting her physician. In one month she was having debilitating hot flashes, became very irritable, and complained that sex was painful. She saw her doctor at my recommendation and he explained the risks and pros and cons of staying on HRT. After weighing the alternatives, she opted to go back on HRT and was soon her old self again.

Another published study indicated a slightly higher risk for breast cancer in women who used HRT. The January 26, 2000, article in the *Journal of the American Medical Association* by Schairer and others compared breast cancer risk in over 46,000 women

Recommended Websites

www.womens-health.com
www.power-surge.com
www.menopause-online.com
www.menopause.org

interviewed between 1973 and 1995, identifying 2,082 cases of breast cancer. The study found that women who were current users, or who had used hormone replacement in the four years prior to diagnosis, had a higher risk of breast cancer than women who had not used hormone replacement therapy. The risk was higher in women who were on the combined estrogen/progestin combination than on estrogen alone.[15]

There is a confusing variety of hormone combinations, types, sources, and routes of administration. That is why you need a trusted doctor or gynecologist who will spend the time to explain the reasons for their recommendations. Read all you can on this topic and be an informed consumer. Talk to your friends and family, but *remember* that menopause is as individual as you are and what is right for your girlfriend may not be right for you. Also bear in mind that what is right for you may change over time. Don't forget to ask God for insight on this very important topic. He has promised to give us wisdom if we ask (James 1:5).

Nonhormonal therapies are available to reduce the symptoms of menopause as well. They include the use of soy products, lubricants, and vitamin supplements such as isoflavones and black cohosh for hot flashes, gingko biloba and vitamin B complex for memory problems, ginseng for fatigue, vitamin E for vaginal dryness, melatonin or chamomile tea for sleep, calcium and vitamin D for bone health, and dong quai for mood swings.

Your lifestyle choices can also affect menopause. Smoking further increases the risk of heart disease and lung cancer. Nutrition plays an important part in continuing health. Diets low in fats and cholesterol and high in vegetables, fruits, and whole grains will help you stay healthy. Alcohol and caffeine intake should also be moderated or eliminated. Exercise helps maintain your physical and mental health.

As you can see, God has uniquely orchestrated our hormones, and understanding the balance between them can make all the difference to a happy and healthy life.

Life is not made up of every breath we take, but by the moments that take our breath away. Staying healthy sexually can help you be breathless each day of your life.

Points to Consider

1. Estrogen, progesterone, and testosterone are all hormones secreted in a woman's body.
2. These hormones all decrease with age—from age twenty on to menopause.
3. Sexually speaking, estrogen is responsible for maintaining the nourishment and moisture of the vagina. Testosterone is the hormone that causes desire in women and stimulates sensitivity to the nipples and clitoris.
4. Sexual desire may change during premenstrual times, pregnancy, breast-feeding and around menopause due to fluctuations in hormones.

5. Women from age thirty on can experience symptoms of perimenopause or menopause.
6. Definite physical changes occur with menopause, differing in intensity among women.
7. HRT is an effective strategy for relieving menstrual symptoms but is not right for all women.
8. Experts disagree on whether HRT increases risks of breast cancer and heart disease.
9. There are effective nonhormonal therapies available for menopausal symptoms. Lifestyle choices also affect menopause.
10. Lack of estrogen can cause painful intercourse. Lowered testosterone can cause lack of sexual desire and decreased sensitivity of the nipples and clitoris.
11. There are local preparations of estrogen and testosterone that can be used which will only be locally absorbed.
12. Reading everything available, knowing the risk factors, talking with other supportive people, praying about the matter, and a thorough discussion with a woman's health care provider will generate the best possible decision for a woman regarding her hormonal balance.

PART III

The Complexity of Sex

CHAPTER 8

LOSS OF DESIRE

The sexual embrace can only be
compared to music and prayer.
HAVELOCK ELLIS

Sex is flaunted more and more in the media and practiced less and less at home. In a recent Kinsey Institute Poll of 853 women, ages twenty to sixty-five, 24.4 percent reported marked distress about their sexual relationship. The phenomenon of loss of desire among young professionals now has an acronym—DINS—meaning, *dual income, no sex!* Obviously, that figure doesn't even take into account the impact having children makes on the frequency of lovemaking.[1] Additionally, time pressure, stress, anger, one partner having an affair, substance abuse, and sexual abuse can all lead to loss of desire.

Hindrances to Desire

If a woman has children and works outside the home she really has two full-time jobs. Even if a husband is helpful, a woman probably still feels that the major household chores rest on her shoulders. Women feel guilty about leaving their kids if they are at work and feel guilty about leaving work if they are at home. With chauffeuring the kids to softball, ballet, soccer, and tutors, there isn't much time left just to feed the kids and get them to bed, let alone have some quality one-on-one time with her husband. Even Dr. Phil is calling the loss of desire an epidemic.

Women today are more knowledgeable about sexuality and want to enjoy it as much as their husbands. This means that a woman may need adequate foreplay time to become aroused. If her husband isn't willing to give her that time, then a woman may feel that sex is just one more thing on her already too full "to do" list.

Many times a woman who goes to bed and is fast asleep before her husband gets out of the shower may be saying no to sex nonverbally. The no may be related to sex (she caught him with a *Playboy* magazine) and she wants nothing to do with him tonight. Or it may not be related to sex at all, such as, the stepson was rude to her and wasn't made to apologize. Sometimes the day-to-day busyness and details of life just get in the way. Someone close to me noted that many couples spend too much time *with* each other but not enough time really *together*. The urgent things—errands, bills, and dirty laundry—demand a woman's attention while the important things—intimacy and closeness—get pushed to the back burner.

Normal sex is whatever a woman and her husband are happy with. Frequency of sex has nothing to do with satisfaction of sex.

Sensual Spoilers: Checklist for Loss of Desire or Blocked Orgasm

1. Medications that impair orgasm
2. Alcohol and nicotine intake
3. Hormonal problems
4. Vaginal or urethral infection
5. Time pressure/stress/sleep deprivation (less than eight hours per night)
6. Husband's emotional or physical affairs
7. Substance abuse
8. Previous sexual abuse
9. Depression
10. Not spending adequate bonding time with husband
11. Ignorance regarding spirituality and sexuality
12. Guilt
13. Problems in relationship with husband:
    - Unresolved anger issues
    - Husband's use of pornography
    - Body image problems
14. Pain
    - Muscle spasms at opening of vagina
    - Infection of any area of the vulva
    - Low cervix/long penis
    - Hormone deficiency
15. Eating Disorders

However, problems can start when the husband wants sex more often than the wife does or vice versa.

The Effects of Anger, Time Pressure, and Stress

Cliff and Michelle came to see me after they had been married for four years. Cliff wanted sex nightly and, in the beginning of their marriage, Michelle had been happy to oblige. However, their finances had gotten tight and Michelle had gone back to work six months after their child was born. She was a CPA with a large firm and had long hours and a great deal of responsibility. Cliff owned his own law firm and was busy as well, but "never too busy for sex," as he put it. Michelle complained of fatigue and stress and stated she no longer wanted to keep up with their nightly love-making. Cliff was disappointed and angry, and even suspected that she was interested in someone at work. And even though both of them were committed Christians, Michelle was furious that Cliff could even suggest the possibility of another man.

When I spoke to Michelle alone she stated she had been angry that Cliff wasn't more helpful around the house since she'd gone back to work. She admitted that part of her loss of desire could have been from anger and fatigue. She also felt like Cliff was subtly (and not so subtly) pressuring her for sex and trying to make her feel guilty when she said no.

When I talked to Cliff he was also angry and felt that Michelle took on too many other things that added to her fatigue. Michelle was singing in the choir at church, taught Sunday school, and helped out with her sister's Brownie troop whenever they needed an extra pair of hands.

It was clear to me that there was some unresolved anger that was fueling the fire. I encouraged Michelle to be very honest and tell Cliff of the resentments that were bothering her. She described her anger over his not helping around the house and her feeling that he was subtly pressuring her for sex with guilt.

When I asked Cliff to rephrase what Michelle had just stated, he ably responded and got it exactly right after two tries. He admitted he had been pressuring her. He realized that was unfair and promised to stop, but he also stated he had no idea that Michelle needed extra help since she appeared to be handling the housework fine on her own.

Michelle admitted she had some problems with being too self-sufficient and that most likely she hadn't been clear in asking for Cliff's help. As we talked, she made it clear that she needed his help with the laundry and with dinner—either cooking dinner or cleaning up afterwards. He was willing—and even offered to cook and clean up on Wednesdays after he finished with his weekly golf outings.

Cliff then told Michelle that he felt lower on her priority list than all her church jobs and the Brownie troop. He asked her to cut back to one job at the church instead of two and to tell her sister she'd have to find other help. Michelle was willing to give up singing in the choir since that would free up one extra night for her to be home. She loved her Sunday school class and wasn't willing to let that go. She agreed to tell her sister to start looking for a different substitute, but said she would continue to help her until she found a replacement.

With the anger issues resolved, Cliff, Michelle, and I moved into the sexuality issues. Michelle wasn't willing to go back to nightly sex. She explained how much she loved Cliff, but now that she was older, working, and taking care of their child, she thought four times a week for sex would be what she could manage.

I taught them the verbiage of different kinds of sex to help them negotiate what they would be willing to do for each other.

Quickie. This is penile vaginal sex, or climax with manual stimulation. It is intended to give sexual release to the person with the greater frequency need. The partner with the lesser need can opt for this if they don't want to spend a lot of time on sex, but want to help their partner out.

No-frills sex. This is sex where both people have an orgasm but there are no frills. It is sex that satisfies both partners, but no extras.

Gourmet sex. This is sex with all the trimmings: candles, music, massage, bathing together, etc. and anything else that will make it a feast.

I also stressed the need for date night every week with just the two of them. This meant no children along, and no double dating so they could share some quality time without being rushed or feeling like they had to entertain someone else.

I explained to them my concept of date night. Many couples think it means fast food and a movie. That might be fun, but it leaves out emotional connecting. Date night should be cozy dinner dates with candlelight and soft music if possible. Showering and shaving, dressing up, and wearing cologne all help the atmosphere to turn intimate later on. Talk about how nice each other looks, why you love one another, what special things that were done that the other spouse really appreciates, a few things you love about each other, and your hopes and dreams.

Date night should not include discussions about the finances, in-laws, work problems, chores, what the other person has done that you don't like, therapy, or other problems. It's meant as a time to bring people together, not push them apart.

In addition to date night, I encouraged Michelle to take a multivitamin, get some healthy exercise a few times a week (walking for thirty minutes and perhaps some weight training), and to begin getting eight hours of sleep per night. She needed to begin taking better care of herself.

With all this in mind, both parties stated what they'd like. Michelle indicated that she would like gourmet sex two nights, but the other two nights she'd be satisfied with a quickie and a no-frills time of sex. Cliff said he'd be happy with four nights a week, and he didn't care what type it was. He wanted Saturday to be date night so Michelle could get a nap during the day and not be tired for their date. He clearly expressed that he wanted date night to end in sexual intimacy. She agreed, especially when he offered to babysit during her nap.

In the following weeks I was pleased to see that Cliff was being even more helpful than he'd agreed to be, and Michelle looked more rested and happy. We terminated counseling with their solemn vow to keep their lines of communication open and to continue their date night commitment no matter what.

The Long-Term Effects of Sexual Abuse

Sexual abuse can be another cause for loss of desire. Women who were sexually abused in the past are more likely to have a lack of interest in sex and can suffer from depression, anxiety, substance abuse, and low self-esteem.

Jana came to see me complaining of loss of desire. She was thirty-two years old and had been married to Phil for ten years. She was aware of early life incest from her stepfather but thought it wasn't a problem until her stepfather moved back to town. Once he did, she began having dreams and flashbacks of the abuse and had suddenly lost all interest in sex with Phil.

I began by asking Phil to be understanding and give us time to work through some of the abuse issues. I taught Jana how this abuse had affected her psychological and sexual development. Then I helped her to grieve the losses caused by the abuse. She was doing fine until one day Jana came in on an emergency basis.

"I've been lying to you all along, Dr. Shay," she said. "The abuse really happened, but there was more to it than I told you. Sometimes I had an orgasm when my stepfather abused me. I feel like my body betrayed me and I'm so ashamed. Since my stepfather came back to town, it's all flooding back and I'm feeling overwhelmed by the memories. Every time I think of sex or orgasm my mind goes right to the abuse."

My heart broke for her as I explained that having an orgasm with abuse was more common than she thought. I also clarified that an orgasm was a reflex, similar to when the doctor hit her knee with a rubber mallet and the lower leg jumped up. I helped Jana to see that, as a twelve-year-old girl, her body was acting in a reflexive way when her abuser touched her. I stressed that any woman in her situation could have had an orgasm with enough clitoral stimulation. She didn't choose her response, just like she didn't choose to be abused.

We discussed how she had been "sexualized" and given carnal knowledge much earlier than God intended. Her feelings of responsibility for this heinous abuse were keeping her imprisoned, far away from her God-given sexual birthright.

Over time, Jana was able to let go of the false feelings of guilt and shame. She realized that she was guilty of *nothing;* while the abuser was guilty of *everything*. It took months to process, but eventually she was able to separate her sexuality from her abuse.

It was a slow process, but Phil stood by her and didn't pressure her for sex while she healed. After eight months of counseling Jana felt as though she could slowly begin working on their sexual relationship again.

At this time I taught her relaxation exercises she could do when she began to feel anxious. I also made her a Scripture tape of verses that pertained to peace and restoration. Sexual abuse taints the perceptions of the mind, but God's truth can renew and transform it (Rom. 12:2). Some of the verses were:

"I will repay you for the years that the locusts have eaten" (Joel 2:25).

"The Lord is with me, I will not be afraid" (Ps. 118:6).

"I, even I, am he who comforts you" (Isa. 51:12).

"Can a mother forget the baby at her breast . . . ? Though she may forget, I will not forget you! See, I have engraved you on the palms of my hand" (Isa. 49:15).

"Never will I leave you; never will I forsake you" (Heb. 13:5).

"Do not be afraid, for I am with you" (Isa. 43:5).

" 'For I know the plans I have for you,' declares the Lord, 'plans to prosper you and not to harm you, plans to give you hope and a future' " (Jer. 29:11).

Jana used both the tape and exercises. As she taught her body how to really relax, she renewed her mind with truth.

I decided to start Jana and Phil on sensate focus exercises described earlier in chapter six. I encouraged her to do the relaxation training before each massage. They began with just having Phil give her a massage at night with her clothes on, but no genital massage. When she could comfortably enjoy that, they progressed to massages with her underwear on but again no genital massage. She was able to reciprocate this massage after a few weeks with no anxiety. Then they advanced to a naked massage with no genital touching. This took longer for Jana to be able to do without anxiety, but with prayer and Phil's patient and loving manner, she accomplished it. Finally, she was able to proceed to genital touching, intercourse, and even after time, orgasm. God had restored her to sexual wholeness and happiness, but it had not come easily or quickly.

At our last visit she teasingly told me she had a present for me. With tears in her eyes she gave me a stainless steel, rubber-tipped doctor's reflex hammer.

"Just so you'll have the real thing," she said, "for the next woman who has been to hell and back."

She moved away a short time later, but I still have my doctor's hammer to remind me of her courageous work and journey.

Sexual abuse victims can have distorted attitudes about sexuality. They might not even be aware of these damaging attitudes until they're introduced by a therapist or pastoral counselor. Jana had come to see her sexuality as a gift from God and was able to let go of her unhealthy and hurtful attitudes toward intimacy.

The Effects of Substance Abuse

In addition to the pressures of time, stress, and sexual abuse, substance abuse can be a cause for loss of libido. It has been reported that occasional marijuana use increases libido temporarily, but with

UNHEALTHY SEXUAL ATTITUDES	HEALTHY SEXUAL ATTITUDES
Sex is an obligation	Sex is a choice
Sex is addictive	Sex is a natural drive
Sex is hurtful	Sex is nurturing and healing
Sex is a condition for love	Sex is an expression of love
Sex is secretive	Sex is private
Sex is exploitive	Sex is respectful
Sex benefits one person	Sex is mutual
Sex is unsafe	Sex is safe
Sex is power over someone	Sex is empowering
Sex is evil	Sex is a gift of God[2]

chronic use, there is a definite *decrease* in desire. Sexual impairment can be caused by chronic use of narcotics, hypnotics, barbiturates, GHB, heroin, and cocaine.

June was a thirty-eight-year-old anesthesiologist who came to see me for loss of desire. I sent her to her gynecologist and everything checked out fine. All her hormones were within normal levels and she had no physical impairments. She was pretty and trim and had no aversive feelings toward her body, so I ruled out any body image problems. She stated she loved her husband and was attracted to him. She denied any unresolved issue or anger. We went over any medications, vitamins, or over-the-counter medications that she could be using that would impair her desire. Nothing was amiss. She denied any sexual abuse, anorexia or bulimia, depression, diseases, or any surgery. She stated she had no pain when they did have intercourse, but she just could not get aroused.

June and her husband were started on sensate focus exercises. At our next meeting June reported no sensuous feelings even though her husband had massaged every inch of her body including her genitals. At this point I was stymied. Her husband was frustrated and I was perplexed. And then it hit me.

I asked her husband to wait in the lobby while I finished up with June. After he left, I asked June if she were using any illegal substances which she was hesitant to tell me about. After fifteen minutes of coaxing, she finally confessed she had smoked marijuana every night for the last twenty years. I explained to her that her sexual problem would get no better if she continued smoking marijuana. She left saying she would call me if she decided to stop, but I have never heard from her again.

The Devastation of Affairs

Another heartbreaking cause for loss of desire is infidelity on the part of your spouse. An affair strikes at the core values of a good marriage—honesty, trust, intimacy, friendship, and commitment. Even if the affair is purely emotional, both partners suffer untold problems. An old pastor I once knew always said, "Never have a best friend of the opposite sex, unless it's your husband."

Many times I've counseled two couples who were best friends. Somewhere in the friendship, the wife of the first couple and the husband of the second couple got together and ended up having an affair.

Mary Lou was a client who initially came in for loss of desire, secondary to marital problems. Her husband, Jim, owned an insurance company and she was a stay-at-home mom of two little girls. Jim worked long hours and even brought work home. She usually fell asleep long before he came to bed. If he did wake her up for sex she felt used and didn't enjoy it at all. After a while, if he wanted to make love when she was fresh and not tired, she recognized that she was angry at him rarely being home. She complained that she felt like a single parent since he even went to work on Sundays and left her to cart three kids to church alone.

When they did talk it was mostly about his agency. She started to hear the name Katie crop up more and more. Katie was a new underwriter they'd hired and Jim sang her praises often. Mary Lou confronted him repeatedly about his and Katie's relationship and he always said it was strictly business. There was that nagging doubt in Mary Lou's mind that something wasn't quite right, but she wasn't sure just what. Over time Jim became irritable with Mary Lou, started telling her she should lose weight, and never approached her anymore for sex.

One day Mary Lou got a call from a church friend. She said she didn't know how to tell Mary Lou, but the friend had seen Jim, the evening before, at a restaurant on the outskirts of town. He was holding hands with a cute brunette and looking longingly into her eyes. Mary Lou was devastated, yet at the same time relieved to know; she had sensed something wasn't right.

That evening she confronted Jim about the incident. Jim initially denied any wrongdoing, but finally broke down and confessed that he'd had an affair with Katie that had started with a one-time fling. He said he had been feeling confused, desperate, and self-loathing lately, but didn't know what to do. He begged for her forgiveness and promised to end the relationship with Katie immediately. He began coming to counseling with Mary Lou and, true to his word, ended the affair. However, a major bone of contention was that he would not fire Katie for fear of a sexual harassment suit.

Both partners experience loss, pain, and guilt after an affair. Both enter a grieving process. The unfaithful spouse sometimes grieves the loss of the affair. The betrayed spouse grieves the security and trust that was broken. They both need to grieve and reclaim their marriage. It's important to define what needs the spouse had that he perceived the affair was trying to meet. How did the love grow cold for the marital partner? When did their intimacy start having weeds grow up around it?

Mary Lou asked detailed questions such as: When did you meet? How many times were you together? What specifically did you do? What positions did you use? I was concerned that knowing all the gory details would be counterproductive to healing and would create visual images that she might never be able to exhume.

The betrayed spouse needs to ventilate feelings of anger, sadness, and fear that the affair brought about. They need to feel that all secrets are destroyed and that the spouse is atoning for the sin committed.

The normal process of grieving is entered into as the couple faces denial, depression, anger, bargaining ("if only I'd . . ."), and acceptance. The spouse who has been betrayed may go over and over the same questions. They may rail at the spouse and start many sentences with "How could you . . . ?" Trust is lost and if the offending spouse is even fifteen minutes late the betrayed spouse may think he is having another affair. The offending spouse has to be scrupulously honest and call anytime they are going to be late.

Both can grow tired of the process of grieving, wanting it to all be over. But the offending spouse needs to realize it takes time to earn back the trust of the betrayed spouse. You can lose trust in an instant, but you earn it back only a little at a time. The recovery stage can take many forms and be different for various couples.

If both husband and wife want to restore the marriage, with God's help it will succeed. Spouses learn more about each other, God's forgiveness and grace, and the process of healing if they can weather the storm.

> You can lose trust in an instant, but you earn it back only a little at a time.

Jim and Mary Lou went through a long and arduous counseling experience. Jim admitted he felt angry at Mary Lou for not giving him enough attention. He felt Mary Lou was too controlling and bossy. Since Jim was never home, Mary Lou admitted she did run the show. She had a habit of telling Jim what they would be doing instead of asking for his input. But she claimed that had only begun after he started working all the time.

Jim had married a woman a lot like his mother whom he described as very controlling. I helped Jim see that his anger was in part toward Mary Lou and in part toward his mother. He had projected his angry feelings toward his mother onto Mary Lou and was partly acting out his anger at Mom by hurting Mary Lou.

Mary Lou had been enmeshed with her children and had put their needs ahead of Jim's. She had poured herself into motherhood since her mother had always worked and never been there for her. She felt justified in doing so because she characterized Jim as a workaholic. Jim explained that he only started staying at work longer and longer hours because he was feeling painfully rejected as he watched Mary Lou catering to the kids and ignoring him.

So which came first—the chicken or the egg? Did Jim's continuing overtime drive Mary Lou to ignore his needs and get her needs met by the kids? Or did Mary Lou's enmeshment with the kids drive Jim to begin working later and later? Each person's perception is their own reality. Jim's reaction to his perceived rejection was to withdraw and get his attention needs met by Katie. Mary Lou's perceived feelings of rejection caused her to withdraw from Jim and attempt to get her needs for quality time and attention met by her kids.

Jim needed more of Mary Lou's attention and appreciation. Mary Lou needed more of Jim's quality time and consideration. Once they began to see what intimacy needs they both had, they were more apt to be aware and willing to meet those needs. Mary Lou also wanted Jim to resume going to church and praying nightly with her like they had done years before. I gave them a copy of the "mini-vows" (described in chapter three) and asked them to end each prayer time with those vows. They agreed. I felt it was important for them to remember what it was that they had vowed to God and each other. Only God's grace and Jim's loving consistency and willingness to keep working on the marriage helped convince Mary Lou not to divorce him.

Jim stopped working eighty-hour weeks, and Mary Lou started making time for Jim in her everyday life. When he came home they would go for a walk and talk over their day and share their feelings. They began having date nights and really started talking about what they wanted and needed from each other. Their intimacy deepened and, over time, the marriage was stronger than it had ever been before. Mary Lou, however, was still not comfortable with sexual intimacy, even though Jim had been tested for all sexually transmitted diseases. Sexual intimacy was the last step of trust that Mary Lou had to take. And Jim finally fired Katie. Soon after, Mary Lou was willing to resume sexual relations with him.

After a year of counseling, their intimacy was resumed and their love life was better than ever. They guarded their relationship more than they ever had before, knowing what the cost of not doing so would be to lose it. As of this writing, they have just welcomed home a little baby boy that was conceived and created in love.

When a Man Loses Desire

All generalizations aside, sometimes it's the husband who does not desire sex. Just as when it's the wife who is experiencing loss of desire, all physical problems must be ruled out by a qualified urologist, especially one who specializes in sexual dysfunction. Sexually transmitted diseases, alcohol or drug addiction, thyroid problems, infections, vascular problems, cancer, diabetes, hormonal abnormalities, and medications are just some of the physical problems that can inhibit desire in men.

A man may experience desire, but be unable to get an erection sufficient for intercourse (erectile dysfunction) or be unable to exercise any control over his ejaculation process (premature ejaculation). Another common problem in orgasm is the male's inability to reach ejaculation (retarded ejaculation). The cause of this can be the misuse of alcohol or drugs since they can depress the nervous system. Another cause of retarded ejaculation can be taking antidepressants, which inhibit ejaculation in men.

Psychological causes for lack of desire in men include fatigue, unresolved conflicts, harbored anger, stress, unmet personal needs, poor communication, and emotionally growing apart.

Early life traumas may be a cause for arousal difficulties. A man may shy away from sex because of the issues it raises emotionally and psychologically. The abuse may need to be processed and explored with a competent therapist.

In addition to the physical issues, sexual dysfunctions commonly produce depression and performance anxiety, particularly in men. If a woman's husband expresses a loss of desire or has any sexual dysfunction, the wife may feel unattractive or unloved.

Whatever the causes for loss of desire, it's vital to treat your sexual relationship like a garden. Don't neglect it—and don't hesitate to get help. The weeds can grow up and choke the flowers, but with daily pruning, weeding, nourishing, and watering, your garden of love can be the most glorious handiwork that God ever made.

Points to Consider

1. Time pressure, stress, anger, affairs, substance abuse, and early life sexual abuse can all lead to loss of desire.
2. Frequency of sex has nothing to do with satisfaction of sex.
3. Learning a vocabulary for different kinds of sex can help a couple compromise and negotiate regarding frequency of sex.
4. Sensate focus exercises can help a couple have less anxiety and get in touch with their sensuous feelings.
5. Tension can be a big obstacle to intimacy, but a woman can benefit from learning relaxation exercises.
6. Illegal drugs, especially used chronically, can result in a loss of desire and orgasmic disorder.
7. It is important to guard your marriage at all times. That is why date night and spending quality time together daily is so vital. It's the little foxes that spoil the vines.
8. Recovery from an affair takes a terrible toll on *both* partners.

CHAPTER 9

Help! I Can't Have an Orgasm!

You may be disappointed if you fail,
but you are doomed if you don't try.

Beverly Sills

Gail was restless and brooding about something she'd gone over thousands of times before in her head. *What's wrong with me? Why won't my body do what I want it to? Are you there God? Who can I ask for help? I need answers for this problem but I'm embarrassed to talk about it.*

Gail finally came to see me after she opened up to a friend who gave her my number. She was tearful, uncomfortable, and finally confessed, "I'm having trouble having an orgasm."

She said her husband was also frustrated because he wanted her to enjoy sex as much as he did, but neither of them knew what was wrong. His feelings of frustration and inadequacy only made Gail feel more pressured to perform and less able to do so.

Gail suffers from what is commonly called Female Orgasmic Disorder or FOD. In *The Hite Report,* a nationwide study of female sexuality, it was reported that 70 percent of women have at some time in their lives been unable to have an orgasm.[1] Those statistics have proven true in my own private practice as a psychotherapist and sex therapist.

Gail didn't realize that orgasm is an inborn capacity, but various factors can block that inborn capacity from being realized. I assured her that she could blast through those blockages with knowledge and skill. I explained that an orgasm is perfectly natural but is rarely naturally perfect!

Just as an orgasm is natural for men, it is also just as natural for women. It is an instinctive, God-given response every woman can achieve. In Genesis 2:24, 25 we read that "a man will . . . be united to his wife, and they will become one flesh. The man and his wife were both naked, and they felt no shame." This total oneness allowed a spiritual, physical, and emotional connection. Sex was a sensational celebration with no performance anxiety, pain, inhibitions, or technique deficits.

The truth is that God is pleased when his children celebrate and enjoy their mutual intimacy. The apostle Paul tells us that sexual intimacy between a husband and wife is actually a picture of the intimacy between Jesus Christ and the church (Eph. 5:28–32). Sex is not only special—it is sacred.

So let's look at the blockages that can occur in our orgasmic quest. Because orgasm involves the mind and the body, the blockages can be physical or psychological in nature.

> Sex is not only special—it is sacred.

Physical Blockages to Orgasm

First, I sent Gail to her doctor for a full gynecological checkup. Gail reported that she had been having intermittent periods and that her mother had had an early menopause. Her doctor found her to be perimenopausal with low testosterone and prescribed a testosterone topical gel. She applied the gel to her vulva (the external part of the genitals) every night. After two weeks, she cut back to a much smaller dose and continued to use it nightly.

Gail's doctor also changed her birth control pill to a triphasic pill, which gives three different levels of progestin at different points through the month, causing less suppression of testosterone. After three months she was able to enjoy all the benefits of intimacy and was grateful for the intervention.

Pain as a blockage to orgasm is one of the most common complaints about sex reported to gynecologists. Pain can be caused by a vaginal or urethral infection, estrogen depletion, muscle spasms at the opening of the vagina, or the formation of a supersensitive bundle of nerves after an episiotomy. Some women experience pain from the penis bumping into the cervix or uterus.

Fortunately, there are medical solutions to most of these problems. Vaginal and urinary infections are easily cured with antibiotics. Estrogen and testosterone levels can be checked and balanced out. Muscle spasms at the opening of the vagina can be

Top Ten Ways Orgasm Benefits a Woman

1. Tightens all perineal (pelvic floor) muscles, preventing incontinence later in life.
2. Increases a brain chemical that elevates mood.
3. Releases a relaxing/bonding chemical, oxytocin, in the brain.[3]
4. Discharges sexual tension.
5. Increases further sexual desire; what you don't use, you lose.
6. Increases lymphocytes that fight infection.
7. Burns 200–300 calories per lovemaking session.
8. Orgasm maintains estrogen levels.
9. Increases endorphins, those feel-good chemicals.
10. It is the ultimate physical union shared with a mate.[4]

treated by desensitizing the vagina. To do this, sex therapists prescribe the use of graduated dilators to gently stretch the opening of the vagina. With the help of a patient partner, this can be cured in 80 percent of such cases.

Feeling a bumping sensation occurs in some women who have a turned cervix or whose husband's penis is unusually large. The pain usually can be alleviated by using a sexual position that changes the direction of thrust.

Sometimes the pain has a more serious cause. Jane was a client who came to see me nine months after her baby was born. She complained of severe pain on the lower edge of her vagina each time she had intercourse. I suspected that Jane had a neuroma—a bundle of extraordinarily sensitive nerves near her vagina. Her gynecologist confirmed my suspicions. He had Jane try several different kinds of creams and ointments (Vitamin A&D, cortisone ointment, lidocaine gel), but nothing removed the pain. She eventually had minor surgery to remove the neuroma. Six weeks later she could handle being touched, and after four months she was orgasmic and pain free.

The first line of defense in breaking through the physical blockage to orgasm is a thorough exam by a good gynecologist, preferably one who specializes in sexual dysfunctions and has knowledge about what can cause the problem.

The second line of defense is examining lifestyle choices. Smoking can damage blood vessels throughout the body, including the genital area. Just as a man's penis gets engorged with blood when aroused, so the female genitals get engorged with blood upon arousal. The nicotine and other chemicals in cigarettes can constrict blood flow to the genitals and thus block orgasm.

Many people find that one to two alcoholic drinks may lessen inhibitions and anxiety so that libido increases. After more than two drinks, however, alcohol impairs orgasm. Alcohol can dampen arousal and delay orgasm because it slows down the central nervous system.

Many medications also can impede or delay orgasm. Antidepressants, blood pressure medication, tranquilizers, narcotics, and even anticholesterol agents can cause low desire, arousal difficulties, diminished genital sensitivity, and can hinder orgasm.

Psychological Blockages to Orgasm

If the physical and lifestyle areas of a client's life check out fine, I consider potential psychological difficulties. Dynamics such as stress, anger, depression, or guilt need to be considered.

Anita was a beautiful woman who thought her marriage was ideal. Then one evening she found her husband viewing Internet pornography when he thought she was asleep. Anita suddenly lost the ability to have an orgasm. Even though she tried, she was unable to feel that complete openness with her husband and no longer was able to respond sexually.

We dealt first with Anita's feelings of betrayal and mistrust. Thankfully, her husband appeared very remorseful and was willing to be involved in therapy. He chose to see a male therapist to work on his personal issues. In spite of his good efforts, every time they had sex, Anita wondered if she was meeting his needs. Her mind was filled with thoughts of, *Is he thinking of those girls on the Internet? Will he do it again? Where had I gone wrong?* These negative thoughts distracted her from being able to enjoy the moment.

Up to this point, Anita had been in denial that their relationship was less than ideal. Now was the time to look at some of the problems that had prompted her husband's voyeuristic behavior.

Anita and John were communicating less and less, and their intimate time together was slipping away. Since Anita was fine with sex once every two weeks, she rarely initiated sex and usually waited for John to do it. This led John to believe she wasn't attracted to him and he felt rejected.

John increasingly turned to solitude in his den when Anita was too busy to spend time with him or go out for some fun. Anita had been wrapped up in the new company she had started and thought John was just fine keeping himself busy. The sad fact was that he was occupying himself in a way that was hurtful to Anita and to their marriage.

Communication, as previously discussed, is ultimately important in a relationship. John and Anita realized that they could probably have averted the betrayal through pornography if they had been more honest and open about what they each needed and wanted from each other sexually.

They realized they had both made mistakes, and they continued working on repairing their relationship. John worked on his addiction to pornography. He joined an accountability group at his church and installed a special Internet filter on their computer. Since pornography is a false illusion of intimacy, it was vital that they restored their *true* intimacy as a couple. Our therapy focused on being more emotionally and physically in tune with each other.

We then worked on improving their ability to deal with their anger in a more constructive way. When Anita was angry she would pout and get moody, but give John no feedback as to what was really wrong. That would leave him feeling angry and desirous to retreat from her. Similarly, John would fail to confront her with his feelings. He would use Internet pornography to make himself feel more in control and more powerful, and to escape from his anger. Subsequently, he was discounting Anita's value.

It took months of counseling for John to understand that he had always avoided conflict and rejection from women due to fear of losing them. Anita discovered that she also avoided conflict, and she learned to be able to speak the truth in love when she was angry.

They began spending time together in the evenings sharing their thoughts and feelings from the day. If Anita was insecure or needed reassurance, she was encouraged to ask for it. If John was angry or anxious, he was encouraged to share those feelings with Anita. John kept her updated as to his progress in therapy. They began having devotions together and praying for their marriage regularly. They started taking ballroom dancing lessons and included their lesson in their date night. They began having fun again and realized why they'd fallen in love in the first place.

Throughout this whole process, there were moments of sexual intimacy, but Anita often ended up withdrawing in fear that the pornography habit would begin again. With John's consistent behavior over time, their relationship became more honest. Anita once again was able to trust John and became orgasmic in a relatively regular manner.

The block that had to be broken through was Anita's distrust and fear after such a traumatic betrayal. One could say the first psychological line of defense in breaking through the blockage to orgasm is identifying anger, sadness, and fear, and getting them out in the open with genuineness and vulnerability.

Ephesians 4:15 says, "Speak the truth in love." In this case, loving truthfulness was crucial for the return of intimacy. Then, with patience, forgiveness, and God's help, this marriage was saved.

Depression is another major blockage to orgasm. One of its identifying characteristics is a lack of interest in everything, including sex. Before sexual problems will abate, the problem of depression must be dealt with. A combination of psychotherapy and medication give the person the best results for a cure. Once the mood is elevated, a person's sexual drive returns.

A client named Alexis came to see me for depression. She had been unable to have an orgasm after she was put on an antidepressant. Her doctor told her, "You have to choose, be depressed or be orgasmic, it's your pick."

That just isn't true. I called and asked her doctor if he would consider changing her to a different medication with fewer sexual side effects or add another medication with the antidepressant that reinstates, if you will, the orgasmic ability. He flatly refused.

Finally, I asked him if she could take a lesser dose on the weekend, and he agreed. Alexis cut her dose by half on the weekend, her orgasmic ability returned, and her mood stayed stable.

Always be sure to check with your doctor about medication changes or allow your sex therapist the permission to speak with your doctor for you. In Alexis's case, the first line of defense in breaking through the blockage to orgasm was a correct medication regimen that continued to treat her depression adequately but restored her orgasmic ability.

Guilt from a rigid upbringing or misbeliefs about sex can cause a great deal of fear. Both guilt and fear mount great obstacles to orgasm. Sarah was a missionary's daughter who was taught nothing about sex, except she should never do it before marriage. The walk down the miraculous marriage aisle did not change years of ignorance nor remove her fear of sex. Sarah had taken to going to bed very early hoping her husband would think she was asleep and not bother her for sex. Sex for her was always painful since she could never relax and let herself become aroused or even lubricated. I began very slowly educating Sarah about the basics of sex. I gave her Scripture to help her realize that sex was something right and good, not bad or dirty.

We then worked on relaxation exercises to help Sarah decrease her anxiety. I gave her a tape of Scripture readings set to soothing background music to listen to daily. While she listened to this tape, she was teaching her body how to relax. She also was renewing her mind with God's Word concerning what he wanted for her in her life and marriage.

Sarah's treatment also consisted of sensate focus exercises with her husband to help her focus on her sensuous sensations. (See chapter six for further discussion of these exercises.) Their first homework assignment was to massage each other, without touching genitals until she could be comfortable just being unclothed and giving and receiving massage. Step two was massage with genital touching but no climax. She began to relax and discover which touches she liked and which she didn't. She also began to lubricate and feel some erotic feelings. Next they progressed to one or two thrusts (with lots of lubrication) until she was comfortable with that. Eventually, Sarah was able to enjoy the entire lovemaking session. However, it still took her six more months until she had her first orgasm.

In this case, knowledge regarding sexuality and spirituality and the importance of relaxation were the lines of defense we needed to address to break down the block to orgasm. Once Sarah could fully believe that it was God's will for her to have an abundant sex life, she began to relax. Then her husband's patience and restraint helped her relax even more until her body did just what it was meant to do, share a wonderful orgasm with the love of her life.

In my observation, most women suffer through the pain of not being orgasmic for three to five years before seeking treatment. Ecclesiastes 3 tells us there is a time to mourn and a time to dance. If you've had intimacy problems—you've had your mourning time. Don't wait any longer. Try some of these ideas and seek professional help if you are still struggling. Reclaim your sexual birthright, and I hope you dance.

Points to Consider

1. A thorough physical exam by a gynecologist who specializes in sexual dysfunctions may reveal physical causes for being nonorgasmic. Ask whether a change in birth control pill might be right for you.

2. Good lifestyle choices help a woman achieve regular orgasms. Not smoking and limiting alcohol are particularly important.
3. Identify and resolve anger, sadness, and fear. Talk about these feelings and process them with genuineness and vulnerability. See a counselor if talking with friends and family doesn't help.
4. Be certain your medication is "orgasm friendly" and check with your doctor or pharmacist for other medications that can do the same job without sexual side effects. If not, question your doctor about limited dosages on weekends.
5. Make sure you know what God says about sexuality and spirituality. Check out some good books on the subject—don't just believe everything others tell you.
6. Learn to relax and let your body do what God intended.
7. God doesn't waste anything. He gives us a free gift that feels great and is even good for us.

Sexuality and Seniors

Life isn't a matter of milestones, but of moments.

R. Kennedy

There are about 76 million baby boomers today and half of them are women.[1] Whether they are perimenopausal, menopausal, or postmenopausal there are more women than ever thinking about ways to stay healthy, happy, and sexy.

Only a few decades ago the word *pregnancy* was not allowed on television, and most people thought that menopause was the end of a woman's sexuality. It was thought that the end of a woman's being able to create children was the end of her sexual life.

Benefits to Sex after Menopause

If sexuality was enjoyable before menopause, there is no reason why it shouldn't continue to be satisfying and enjoyable. Since postmenopause relieves any worry of getting pregnant, it can give a woman a new sense of sexual freedom.

Many times the senior age means the departure of grown children. For the first time in years, you can walk around in your underwear if you want to. There is more privacy for intimacy and more freedom to be sexual anywhere in the house you choose.

For some women, not having menstrual periods means they can be sexual all through the month. It may mean more time for intimacy.

After forty, many women feel more sexually assured and secure. They know what they like and are less hesitant to experiment. They can communicate their sexual needs and preferences to their spouses. Many women didn't learn how to have an orgasm until their late twenties or thirties, so the forties are a time when they are more relaxed, more sure of how to have an orgasm, and more sure of how to please their husbands. They continue to grow in their sexual knowledge and have let go of old inhibitions.

Certain physical changes take place, however, that may affect your sexuality.

Physical Factors that Affect Sexuality in Senior Women

Physical body changes and changes in the sexual response cycle are somewhat different for females than for males. The depletion of estrogen and testosterone that comes with age causes changes in the genitalia. The vaginal walls become thinner and the vagina actually decreases in length and width. There is also a reduction in lubrication. Due to the decrease of testosterone, there is a reduction in sexual drive or desire, thinning and loss of pubic hair, less clitoral and nipple sensitivity, and overall decreased capacity for orgasm (see chapter seven for a more in-depth discussion of this topic). Women who had an active sex life before menopause, however, typically do not have as much loss of vaginal elasticity or sexual response.

During the sexual response cycle, arousal may take longer and the lubrication during the excitement phase may be less. The sexual tension that mounts during this stage may be less dramatic. Due to arteries which can be constricted or clogged, there can be a reduced blood flow to the vulva, interfering with arousal. At the time of orgasm, the contractions can be less and many women complain that the orgasm is less intense and less satisfying. The phase after orgasm, the resolution phase, may occur more rapidly for the menopausal woman, but she is still capable of achieving orgasms as in her earlier years.[2]

Doing Kegel exercises (described in detail in chapter five) several times each day helps preserve vaginal muscle tone and prevents bulging or prolapse of the bladder or rectum into the vagina. Having regular sexual relations with your husband also helps to maintain vaginal muscle quality.

Many older people are taking drugs for one illness or another. Blood pressure medication, cardiac meds, antidepressants, diuretics, and benzodiazepines are all common drugs for people over fifty-five and all can contribute to sexual side effects in women and men.

Alcohol is another problem of the baby boomer generation. Since alcohol (more than one drink) depresses the central nervous system, it can result in lower orgasmic ability in women.

Our society reveres youth and beauty, so many seniors feel as if sexuality, also, is only for the young. One couple I worked with, Ginger and Mike, were both in their early sixties. Their teenage grandson had realized that Grandma and Grandpa were still sexual. His comment to Grandpa was, "Yuck, that's just gross." Mike said he suddenly felt like a dirty old man and Ginger felt guilty about being sexual with her husband of thirty-nine years.

We discussed the negative societal myths of equating sexuality with youth. I explained that couples who were sexual lived longer and healthier lives. Some suggest that sexual activity may promote brain function in seniors.[3]

Rather than being embarrassed, I encouraged them to be proud. They were giving their heirs a healthy example and permission to be sexual as they age. Their children and grandchildren would remember what lively and youthful people Ginger and Mike were.

Besides, in a study done by Consumer Reports, 59 percent of men and 65 percent of women who were seventy years of age or older still engaged in sexual intercourse, and half of those had sex once a week.[4]

Psychological Factors that Affect Sexuality and Senior Women

Changes in the marital relationship can be a factor in sexuality and seniors. When either the husband or wife retires or decreases their workload, both people must adapt. For the first time in many years, the couple may be spending long hours together. This can cause some conflict until the system adjusts to the changes. But this conflict, if not resolved correctly, can become one of the biggest hindrances to sexuality. Anger is an especially detrimental emotion when it comes to sexuality. If a woman represses the anger long enough, it can erode her desire like battery acid.

Penny was a sixty-year-old patient who came to see me after she heard a lecture I gave on female sexuality. She'd had a partial hysterectomy and breast removal for cancer and had been on an antidepressant that caused a loss of desire and the inability to have an orgasm. She had gone off the antidepressant six months earlier and felt her mood was fine. However, her loss of sexual desire was not.

One problem was her intense anger at her husband. She felt that he had not been supportive through her surgeries or her sexual problems. Penny and Paul came to see me for therapy. I soon discovered that Paul had been frightened of her dying, so he had withdrawn from her. He couldn't even stand the smell of the hospital without feeling nauseated.

Since Penny's anger was long-standing, it took some time for Paul to convince her of his remorse and even longer for her to forgive him. But eventually, they talked it out and the conflict was resolved.

They began to have sex again. And although Penny was willing to try, she still could not have an orgasm. She continued to have a loss of desire and the inability to have an orgasm. Since Penny wasn't a candidate for hormonal therapies due to her cancers, her doctor ordered Viagra® to increase blood flow to her genital area and increase genital sensation. She was more sensitive right from the start of the medication. She became orgasmic and is doing well.

In Ephesians 5, God directs husbands "to love their wives as their own bodies. He who loves his wife loves himself. After all, no one ever hated his own body, but he feeds and cares for it, just as Christ does the church" (Eph. 5:28, 29). Feeding and caring give the idea of nourishing and cherishing. Retirement gives a man the time to nourish, carefully protect, and *cherish* his wife. Since women have been the cherishers of the family for so many years, it's endearing to a woman now to be the one to be cherished. Having a husband cherish and nourish a woman can certainly ease the stresses of this life change.

God admonishes women to *respect and reverence* their husbands. Ephesians 5:33 in the Amplified Bible admonishes the wife, "that she notices him, honors him, prefers him, venerates and esteems him; and that she defers to him, praises him and loves and admires him exceedingly." Of all the times in life, I believe retirement is the time when a man needs this type of love more than ever. Since a man's job has been so important to him for so much of his life, leaving that job, even for retirement, can be a very difficult transition. His godly wife can ease the conversion to a new stage of life with her love.

While some women feel what Margaret Mead called "menopausal zest," other women feel they are no longer a real woman after menopause. They suddenly think of themselves as old and feel as if their usefulness is over. They remember the days when they weighed 125 and wore a size six, and they feel as if their aging body has betrayed them.

Things may slow down, but it's important for a woman to change her thinking and concepts about herself as a postmenopausal woman. Think about Laura Bush, who is a beautiful lady. She isn't twenty anymore and I doubt she is a size six, but she is beautiful, vibrant, and a wonderful role model for all women. Or what about Sophia Loren? She is a beautiful, sensual woman who has appeared in movies about older couples.

This is a time when a woman can reframe how she thinks about herself. It's a time of quiet beauty, where she can claim her wisdom and ask God to show her his purpose for her at this stage of her life.

Maybe some idea of our purpose as seniors can be found in Titus 2:3, 4, where Paul challenges older women, "to be reverent in the way they live, not to be slanderers or addicted to much wine, but to teach what is good. Then they can train the younger women to love their husbands and children, to be self-controlled and pure, to be busy at home, to be kind, and to be subject to their husbands, so that no one will malign the word of God."

Physical Factors that Affect Sexuality in Senior Males

Men experience significant sexual changes as they age that are important for a woman to be aware of. It is essential for a woman to know about these changes in her husband's body because many men do not share this easily.

As he ages, a man has decreased production of testosterone which then stabilizes around age sixty. The size and firmness of his testicles may be reduced. There is a reduction in sperm. The prostate enlarges and, if there are tumors, surgery may be required.

Ironically, men become more like women sexually as they age. First, they need more direct tactile stimulation, or more foreplay, to get a hard erection. The erection may not be as firm as when a man was younger. A man's erection may be delayed and he may need sensual touch not just visual stimulation. This is hard for most men to admit, because in times past they relied solely on visual stimulation. Secondly, a man may need to thrust a lot longer than he used to in order to ejaculate. This can be an asset for the woman who needs more time and stimulation to help her achieve orgasm. It's essential for a wife to be sensitive to this and not urge her husband to "hurry up." A man also needs more time in between orgasms and may not be able to be ready to have sex again as quickly as he used to be. His orgasm may be shorter and he may not ejaculate with every orgasm.[5]

Maximizing This Stage of Life

Aging does not have to mean the end of your sexual life. In fact, it can be better than ever. Sexuality at this stage of life can be less goal oriented and more process oriented. The journey becomes as important as the destination.

An orgasm doesn't always have to be the end of every sexual encounter, either. Just having foreplay can give a couple a feeling of closeness as seniors. But having some sex play is vital to keeping your sexual fires burning.

Touch is another way to connect. Psychologist Tiffany Field, who directs the Touch Research Institutes at the University of Miami School of Medicine, states that the benefits of touch are shown at almost every age. Touch can slow heart rate, lower blood pressure, increase serotonin levels, and lower the stress hormone cortisol.[6]

Just giving each other a massage can be beneficial to relating and creating intimacy. In a personal interview, licensed massage therapist Nancy Coker stated: "Massage can relax you, improve your circulation, and increase a sense of well-being. Rubbing and massaging each other can help in emotionally connecting you to your mate."

Points to Consider

1. Senior sexuality brings benefits of privacy, ceased menstruation, and no fear of pregnancy.
2. Seniors who are sexual live longer and healthier lives.
3. Senior sexual activity may actually promote brain function.
4. Senior women crave their husband's cherishing and love; senior men crave their wives' respect and reverence.
5. Being a senior woman is a time of quiet beauty where a woman can ask God for wisdom about her purpose during this time of life.
6. Physical changes in the sexual response cycle do occur as women age, but a woman can be proactive and ameliorate those changes.
7. Women who have had an active sex life before menopause typically don't have as much loss of vaginal elasticity or sexual response after menopause.
8. Kegel exercises and regular sexual relations help maintain vaginal muscle quality.
9. Senior men also experience physical factors that affect sexuality.
10. Touch can emotionally bond you to your spouse.

Fifteen Tips for Maximizing Sexuality as a Scintillating Senior

1. Have your hormones checked and discuss any sexual dysfunction with a knowledgeable and empathetic professional.

2. Check any medications you're taking with your local pharmacist and ask if there could be any sexual side effects from them. Don't immediately assume that your sex drive is low because you are getting older. If you are experiencing the potential side effects, have your pharmacist call your doctor and ask for a replacement drug that will have the same action without the sexual side effects.
3. Drinking alcohol should be a no-no. The effects of alcohol can lessen arousal and orgasmic ability. The depressive effects of alcohol can become more pronounced as a person ages.
4. Eradicate any myths from your mind about sex and aging. Sexuality is a healthy, God-given gift that will keep you young and vibrant.
5. If you are having any relationship problems, get to a pastor or counselor and resolve old issues or anger. Compromise. Take turns giving in. Agree to disagree. Conflict is detrimental to your sexuality.
6. If you're having difficulties dealing with retirement, get counseling to resolve those issues. Strive to respect your husband like the Ephesians verses recommended. Ask him to love you like Christ loved the church.
7. Work on loving your body and resolving any body image problems. Look at this time as a spiritual, sexual, and serenity passage. Focus on your strengths. Be creative in finding ways to feel more attractive—get a new hairdo, learn how to use makeup, get acrylic nails.
8. Allow your sexuality to focus more on pleasure than performance. Shift to delighting in the process as much as looking forward to the outcome.

9. Vow to be physical with one another without expecting sex to be the outcome. Cuddle, hold hands, or massage one another. Spend at least fifteen minutes every day touching your mate.
10. Ask God to show you your path and purpose in this exciting stage of life.
11. Stay physically fit. Maintaining a healthy body weight and doing some form of regular exercise can increase your stamina and overall enjoyment of sexual activity.
12. Don't let the presence of medical conditions stop you from being sexual. Read the next chapter on sexuality and illness.
13. Don't smoke. Smoking can reduce blood flow to the genitals.
14. Don't let the fear of discussing sexual issues keep you imprisoned. Find a reputable sex therapist, doctor, or nurse practitioner.
15. Use what you have. What you don't use, you lose.

Sexuality and Illness

Pain nourishes courage.
You can't be brave if you have only
had wonderful things happen to you.
Mary Tyler Moore

Just as in other phases of life, sex is perfectly natural but after illness, it's rarely naturally perfect. When a woman initially hears she has an illness, it puts her into a tailspin. She seems to be suspended in time and life just continues on around her.

A woman wonders how the illness will affect her daily life, her husband and children, her work at home, her job, and her hobbies and leisure activities. It may not be until later that she wonders how the illness will affect her sexually. That may turn out to be one of the most difficult adjustments to make. Early reactions to a new illness are shock, denial and anger, anxiety, and stress.

> Sex is perfectly natural but after illness, it's rarely naturally perfect.

Elizabeth was stunned when she found out at thirty-nine years of age that she had had a heart attack. She was in utter disbelief.

"I couldn't be having a heart attack," she kept saying, "I'm only thirty-nine years old!"

She thought her age protected her from an old-age disease. She came to see me for depression after her heart attack. Her denial of the heart attack was one of the hardest things to deal with. After she eventually came to grips with it, we devised a heart protection plan for prevention of future occurrences. She began exercising daily and worked up a nutrition plan with a dietitian. Because she'd been a workaholic, she cut back to a normal workweek and added in more time for leisure and fun. The plan also included ways to combat her depression through antidepressants and therapy. Using rebuttals of negative self-defeating thoughts with Scripture and other logical statements, she began to practice healthy positive thinking.

Three months after her heart attack she was doing better than she had before. She considered the heart attack a wake-up call to change her life.

Facing the Emotional and Physical Changes

Following treatment for any major illness, the biggest obstacle is accepting what has transpired and facing the uncertainty of what may be coming next. At each step of the way, emotional and physical factors can interfere with a woman's ability to live fully and have an active sex life.

My first goal in therapy is to help a woman think in a different way about sexuality and her illness. Differing disease processes require differing sexual changes—and changes can be frightening. But knowing that there are ways to cope with the changes can help a woman feel optimistic and give her a measure of control. Although there may be changes in her sex life, it's important to realize that sexual pleasure can take many forms.

To combat worry and fear of the unknown, I usually will have a client memorize Philippians 4:6, 7:

> Do not be anxious about anything, but in everything, by prayer and petition, with thanksgiving, present your requests to God. And the peace of God which transcends all understanding will guard your hearts and your minds in Christ Jesus.

I instruct her to use these verses to eject any thoughts of worry or fear when they intrude into her conscious mind.

Many doctors often overlook or superficially deal with a woman's sexuality after she has been diagnosed with a disease. Women suffer needless anxiety regarding their sexuality due to

Websites

www.americanheart.org
www.diabetes.org/main/info
www.nationalmssociety.org
www.webmd.com

inappropriate attitudes or lack of knowledge on the part of the health care provider. In their defense, many doctors were never trained in the area of sexuality, but all patients should be given the opportunity to express their concerns and get the correct answers or a referral to someone who specializes in sex therapy.

Health problems can make sex uncomfortable, cause depression, and drive a wedge between husbands and wives. There are specific sexual coping strategies and approaches to the four major health issues of heart disease, diabetes, multiple sclerosis, and back pain. Cancer brings its own challenges to a woman's sexuality, so we will discuss that separately in the following chapter.

Sexuality and Heart Disease

Heart disease is the leading cause of death among American women today. Two hundred sixty-seven thousand women die each year from heart attacks. That means that six times more women die from heart disease than from breast cancer. Eight million American women are presently living with heart disease.

A few facts about women who are at risk for heart disease:

On average, smokers will die nineteen years earlier than nonsmokers.
Women with diabetes are two to three times more likely to have a heart attack.
Women with high blood pressure are more likely to have a heart attack or stroke.
Women who are obese are more likely to have a heart attack.[1]

Many women with heart disease have a loss of desire and an inability to have an orgasm. The true problem, however, tends to be fear. Many women are desperately afraid to put that much exertion on their heart for fear of bringing on another heart attack. One study revealed that only 0.9 percent of heart attacks occurred within two hours of sexual activity.[2]

Ruth was a sixty-four-year-old woman who had had a heart attack one month prior to seeing me. She came with Stanley, her husband of forty years. Stanley had urged her to come because he was confused and upset about their love life. Ruth was dreadfully afraid of having sex for fear of upsetting her heart and bringing on another heart attack.

We went over Ruth's medications and they seemed to be fine. Ruth explained that sexuality had always been a highlight of her and Stanley's life and that she was able to feel aroused, but she just wouldn't let herself go beyond that point. She had refused to go to cardiac rehabilitation because she was afraid the exertion would bring on another heart attack.

She was more interested in listening when I explained that cardiac rehab would start out gradually and would actually help build up an auxiliary or supplementary blood supply to the heart through exercise. Helping her realize that cardiac rehab was the best way to prevent a heart attack made her willing to go. Then I informed her that having an orgasm was about as stressful as climbing two flights of stairs. When she got to the place in rehab where she could climb two flights of stairs without any chest pain, then her heart was ready for an orgasm. I also encouraged her to ask her doctor if she could take one nitroglycerin tablet before sex to dilate her coronary vessels.

Stanley was excited to hear this and immediately wanted to join the gym so he could exercise with her.

Listed below are some specific facts and methods that will help you adapt your sexual life when dealing with heart disease:

1. The amount of exertion for intercourse and orgasm is equivalent to climbing two flights of stairs without chest pain. If you can climb stairs, you can have sex safely.
2. Take medications such as coronary vasodilators before sex to open up the cardiac blood vessels and prevent pain or spasm.
3. If you have any problems with desire, arousal, or orgasm ask your doctor or pharmacist if any of your medications could have sexual side effects. If they do, ask if there is another medication with the same action but no sexual side effects. Don't just assume the doctor picked the one medication without sexual side effects. At times doctors don't even think of sexual side effects when ordering drugs.
4. The best positions are missionary position with the female on the bottom, or spoons position. These use the least exertion for the female with heart disease.

Sexuality and Diabetes

Diabetes affects 9.1 million women or 8.9 percent of women over the age of twenty in America today. Diabetes is the fourth deadliest disease in the United States, and it has no cure. The risk for diabetic coma is 59 percent higher for women than for men. The sexual problems of diabetic women were not even considered until 1970, although the diabetic males' sexual problems had been studied years before.

At least 7.6 percent of women with diabetes suffer from a condition known as PVD or Peripheral Vascular Disease. PVD is a disorder resulting in reduced blood flow and oxygen to the peripheral or outer parts of tissues of the feet, legs, and pelvis.[3] Sexually,

PVD results in decreased genital sensitivity due to reduced blood flow and oxygen to the vulva.

Women with diabetes can have an increased risk of vaginal infections. One-third of women have vaginal dryness. High blood sugars can cause women to feel fatigued all the time. In the later stages of diabetes, women can get nerve damage to the eyes, hands, vulva, feet, and legs.

Here are some specific facts and methods that will help you adapt your sexual life when you have diabetes:

1. Keeping a tight control on blood sugar is one of the best ways to deter nerve damage. If you are on insulin, speak to your doctor about the insulin pump.
2. Monitor your diet very carefully to keep blood sugar in line. This will promote increased energy since high blood sugar causes fatigue.
3. Blood sugar control will also cut down on the numerous vaginal irritations and yeast infections that can occur.
4. Orgasm can cause blood sugar to fall, so drink some orange juice or take another type of food source with sugar before making love.
5. Use a vaginal lubricant that your pharmacist or doctor recommends which is less likely to cause vaginal infections.
6. Any position that is mutually agreed upon is best.

Sexuality and Multiple Sclerosis

Multiple sclerosis or MS is an autoimmune inflammatory disease of the central nervous system. It is marked by damage to the sheath that covers the nerves. It affects approximately one million young adults, mostly women. MS symptoms can include:

Vision disturbances
Fatigue
Loss of balance and dizziness
Stiff muscles
Speech problems
Bowel and bladder problems
Short-term memory problems
Partial or complete paralysis[4]

Multiple sclerosis can affect a woman's sexuality dramatically. Different physical symptoms can interfere with sex. When these symptoms are in the picture, a woman may avoid talking about the problem or avoid sexual relations altogether. This only makes matters worse. Confiding in one's husband actually deepens intimacy and can go a long way to resolving problems and anxieties about sex. Sexual problems for women with MS include:

Decreased vaginal lubrication
Loss of desire
Numbness or pain in the vulva
Decreased muscle tone
Decreased frequency of orgasm
Bowel and bladder accidents[5]

Here are some specific facts and coping methods that will help you adapt your sexual life when you have MS.

1. Numbness of the vaginal or clitoral area may occur. However, the nerves that sense vibration can be more sensitive than the nerves that sense light touching, so a vibra-

tor may be very helpful with numbness or inability to have an orgasm.

2. Pain is frequently a problem. Make sure to schedule intimacy at the time when your pain medicine will peak. Then it will be easier to make love, pain free.
3. Fatigue can be a problem. Most fatigue problems can be helped by scheduling intimacy in the morning hours when most MS patients are at their best.
4. Spasticity of muscles can be treated with medication, cold packs, massage, or stretching.
5. Decreased lubrication and muscle tone are common. Good lubrication is vital so Astroglide, KY Liquid, or Replens® vaginal suppositories (three times a week) for lubrication are all helpful. Kegel exercises will keep your vaginal muscle tone in good order.
6. Bowel and bladder accidents can be managed through medication and establishing a regular eating and toileting routine. Accidents may happen, but try to keep a positive and humorous attitude about them.
7. If a woman is menopausal, estrogen vaginal cream or testosterone gel can help with dryness and flagging desire.
8. Positions that conserve energy are good. If bowel or bladder problems occur, the female on the bottom may work best as she can lie on some type of absorbent liner. Recommended positions: Side positions or the woman lying on her back with her legs over the man.

When I first began seeing Jennifer she was forty years old and had been diagnosed with MS ten years before. She initially came in for depression, but also said she hadn't been intimate with her husband in years. The last time they had had sex, her legs went into spasm, and she was so disgusted with herself she never wanted to try to have sex again. We began by working through the grief and loss issues the disease had caused. At the same time, we got her started on an antidepressant that had no sexual side effects.

I used a form of therapy where you look at your self-defeating beliefs and make a choice to change them. Thoughts precede feelings and feelings precede behavior, so to change your behavior you need to go back to your thoughts. What you tell yourself is what you become.

Jennifer had been telling herself that she'd never have sex again, her life was over, her husband would eventually leave her, and then she'd die. As she began memorizing positive Scriptures to refute her negativity, she began to get more optimistic. Her favorite verse was Mark 10:27, "All things are possible with God."

Once the medication began to take effect and we started discussing how she could work around her disease and be sexual again, she got excited. Her main sexual problem had been vaginal dryness and the spasticity of her legs.

Jennifer went to her doctor and found out she was perimenopausal. Her doctor put her on a vaginal estrogen cream and increased the medication for spasticity of her muscles. Her husband came in and we developed a plan for sexuality. Since Jennifer got tired easily, I suggested that the morning might be a good time for sex, preferably on a weekend when he was off work and could take his time. Then Jennifer needed to take her medication for spasticity about an hour before they planned to have sex so it could be at its peak. Her husband would massage her leg muscles and she would do some stretching exercises. Then they would use a good lubricant like Astroglide and just let nature take its course.

Jennifer reported she was very anxious the first few times but then she began to relax and soon their sexuality was happening like clockwork every Saturday morning.

Sexuality and Back Pain

Eighty percent of all adults will have lower back pain sometime in their lives. In fact, 6.5 million Americans are treated for lower back pain each day. Lower back pain is the most common cause of disability in people younger than forty-five.

The most common causes of lower back pain are injury, herniated disk, spinal deformities, arthritis, and compression fractures. Back pain can include muscle spasms, cramping, stiffness, and acute or chronic pain. Though this occurs most commonly in the lower back, it can occur in the hips or buttocks as well.

Almost any back pain can cause problems with sex. Back pain can be categorized into four types.

1. One-sided back pain.
2. Extension-type back pain. This type of back pain occurs in the process of bending forward.
3. Flexion-type back pain. This type of back pain occurs in the process of bending backwards.
4. Brittle back pain. This is an advanced state of pain that can tolerate little movement in any direction.[6]

Here are some specific facts and methods that will help you adapt your sexual life when you have back pain.

Plan sex around peak pain relief, peak energy, and peak privacy. Keep a positive attitude and stay as active as possible.

Proper positioning is one of the most important methods to help with back pain problems and sexuality.

For *one-sided back pain*, any position that supports the painful side is good. The side-by-side position or the missionary position are good options.

For *extension* problems, a position that supports arching of the back can be a dramatic help with sexuality. The missionary position with pillows under the back might be helpful.

For *flexion* problems, any position that utilizes bending forward such as bending over a support or spoons with upper back bent forward is the most useful.

For a *brittle back* the best position is lying supine on the bed (face to the ceiling), with pillows under the knees and the head. A small rolled towel can be placed under the low back. The brittle-back woman should allow her husband to do most of the movement and she should lie as still as possible to prevent further pain.

Dealing with a Husband's Pain or Disease

What happens when the husband and not the wife is facing illness or depression? When a woman goes through any situation where her husband's ability to function sexually is impaired it is common for her to feel an entire gamut of emotions. Initially, most women are empathetic and supportive, especially if the problem is erectile dysfunction from surgery or cancer treatment, or any other physical cause.

If the problem continues and the treatment is long and involved, the grief process typically ensues and the woman may have the following normal reactions:

denial—"this can't be happening to us,"
depression—normal sadness and sorrow over the situation,
anger—at the situation, the husband, herself, and anything else she chooses to displace the grief anger onto,
bargaining—"if only he'd . . ." or "if only I'd . . . ," and finally *acceptance.*

If the problem is erectile dysfunction from a psychological cause, a woman will, typically, tend to believe her attractiveness or lack of attractiveness has something to do with the problem. This is usually not true, but many women I've seen in counseling immediately jump to this conclusion. A woman needs to be reassured that this is almost never the case.

A woman also needs to be encouraged and instructed that the most important thing she can do for her husband is be patient and accommodating during this complex time while he works through his issues. This can be very difficult for her to do as she may also be dealing with her own issues of fear, sadness, and anger. A good counselor who can help normalize her feelings and offer coping skills to help during this time can be a wonderful asset.

God never promised there would be no storms in life, but he did promise that he would hold our hands and walk us through those storms. Illness can be one of the most difficult challenges to face, especially if it's chronic illness. But we need to fight to keep our intimacy alive and not give up just because it requires change or some extra measures.

Points to Consider

1. Reactions to illnesses include denial, depression, anger, bargaining, and finally acceptance.

2. Emotional and physical factors can all play a part in a woman's sexuality after an illness.
3. Heart disease is the leading cause of death for women today.
4. Illness can cause depression, pain, fatigue, and sexual dysfunction.
5. Ask your doctor or pharmacist about sexual side effects from your medication if sexual problems arise.
6. Lubrication is frequently needed with many illnesses.
7. Special attention usually needs to be paid to helpful sexual positions when illness is a factor.
8. Be sure to take pain medication and allow it to peak before making love. Pain and orgasm must not coincide.
9. Getting your husband involved in problem solving can make him feel loved and needed.
10. Couples who continue to be sexually active, even during illness, have a greater emotional intimacy.

CHAPTER 12

Sexuality and Cancer

When we long for life without difficulties, remind us that oaks grow strong in contrary winds and diamonds are made under pressure.

Peter Marshall

Sexuality is a basic human need that comes after air, food, water, shelter, and safety. If you were aboard the *Titanic* and you heard it was sinking, it's a sure bet that sex would not be the next thing on your mind. So it is when you are confronting cancer. Initially, most women who are newly diagnosed with cancer aren't worried about their sexuality. Most likely their major concern is self-preservation. But once the roller coaster of feelings begins to settle down, new questions arise.

A patient I treated named Cindy came in tearfully telling me she'd had a mastectomy and couldn't even imagine having sex with her husband again. She was fearful she would never be normal again, and she was even terrified to look at her own scar. She told me that her husband was very supportive, but he was unsure what to do. She had chosen a breast prosthesis instead of opting for breast reconstruction. Her doctor had assured her they had gotten it all, so she was no longer afraid of the cancer killing her—just killing her sex life.

Facing Sex after Cancer

While life may be different, it doesn't have to be bad. A good definition of sex after cancer is this: *Sex is any sexual expression of caring between two consenting adults.*

The true measure of a woman's worth as a lover is the pleasure she and her partner find together. Because of the care and thought that must go into the sexual experience after cancer, sex now becomes a journey, not a destination. It should be savored like Godiva chocolate, not gulped like ice water on a hot day.

> Sex now becomes a journey, not a destination. It should be savored like Godiva chocolate, not gulped like ice water on a hot day.

Cindy was hesitant to discuss sex and embarrassed by the problem. She felt she should just be happy to be alive and not complaining about her sexual problems. She also felt she was a burden to her husband and that her sex life was over forever.

I explained that her feelings were normal in this situation and many people are uncomfortable talking about sex. I also explained that, after the initial denial, shock, anger, anxiety, and surgery, the next big hurdle is acceptance of what had happened and the ability to learn and institute some new changes regarding sex.

I ended our first session explaining that sexuality is vital since it's one glue that holds a marital relationship together. Cindy was letting fear rob her of her need for closeness, touch, playfulness, and caring. We agreed that we would begin by working on her acceptance of the cancer, her surgery, and her grief issues.

I assured Cindy that most sex therapy was sexual education. Since the Bible says that the marriage bed is pure and undefiled (Heb. 13:4), couples have a great deal of latitude in how they express their sexuality. Different attitudes, different positions, and different touches would most likely restore the joy of their sexuality.

Since the scar was such a major focus of Cindy's revulsion, we began by slowly desensitizing her to the scar. I had Cindy look at her scar in the mirror for short periods of time and then for longer and longer intervals as she became more used to its appearance. The more one becomes familiar with something, the more one will eventually accept it. Then I had Cindy begin touching the scar very slowly and only in tiny spots. She then could go on to touching the scar for longer times and in larger areas. She became familiar with the total look and feel of her scar. She began to notice what was numb, what was painful or tender, and what areas felt all right.

In time, I suggested that she might like to have sex wearing her prosthesis, bra, and a camisole. Then her husband wouldn't see the scar or touch it and she could still feel sexy. Cindy liked that idea and, very slowly, she began to have regular sex with her husband again.

The next step was to have sex wearing just the bra and prosthesis, without the camisole. Each step took time, but she was very brave and persevered—to her husband's delight. She finally worked her way to having sex with only the prosthesis on, since she had the kind that could be glued to her body.

After six months of therapy, Cindy was able to talk about showing her husband, John, the scar. She decided she would try it the next time they made love. I was surprised when they both came to my office for her next session. They both wanted to share with me the outcome of her unveiling. Cindy related that, as she removed the prosthesis, they both began to cry. John kissed the tip of his index finger and then very gently touched the scar. Then he continued kissing his fingertip and touching the scar until he had vicariously kissed the whole scar. John then said, "Let's name the scar. Let's call it 'Hero' because it saved your life."

That was one tearful session! I cried, too—with joy and happiness that God had so beautifully brought good out of a potentially threatening experience.

The Challenge of Cancer Treatments

Many clients ask me how cancer will affect their sexuality. I explain that what really affects sexuality are the side effects of the cancer treatments such as surgery, chemotherapy, and radiation.

Surgery can result in pain, body image problems, hormonal differences, lack of desire, orgasmic difficulty, and depression.

Chemotherapy can result in nausea, fatigue, painful joints and skin, lack of desire, and orgasmic difficulty. It can also include reduced hormones, hot flashes, vaginal dryness and inflammation, yeast infections, and hair loss.

Radiation can result in less vaginal moisture, reduced vaginal size, painful intercourse, low sexual desire, and skin irritation.

When Pain Is the Problem

Pain is a major complaint after cancer treatment, as well as one of the most common problems for women who don't have cancer. It's often related to changes in the size or moistness of the vagina.

Good lubrication is vital after most cancer treatments. Many patients don't know that it's important to lubricate both the penis and vagina. If a woman has a loss of estrogen from surgery or any other cause, vaginal estrogen cream can be applied in a tablet or cream into the vagina three times a week. Estrogen nourishes and revitalizes the tissues of the vagina. If a woman cannot have any form of estrogen due to her cancer being estrogen sensitive, Replens® is a product that can be bought over the counter and used by inserting it into the vagina three times a week to nourish and moisturize the vagina. It contains no estrogen but is a good internal lubricant. Replens® can also be a deterrent for vaginal infections since it helps maintain the normal pH of the vagina.

The man can lubricate his penis with a water-based lubricant that does not dry out. Astroglide or Lubrin® are good ones to try. Never use Vaseline or oil-based lubricants as they could cause infection. For severe dryness, one of the lubricating suppositories may be inserted into the vagina just before sex to provide even more lubrication.

Using your old tried-and-true position can sometimes prove to be painful, so new positions need to be tried and evaluated. In my experience, the woman on top position is one of the best positions for reducing pain as it gives the woman the most control. It requires the man to lie on a pillow from his head to his buttocks.

Then, when the woman straddles the man, she can ease in his penis, thereby decreasing pain. She also can control how fast he thrusts and how deep he goes. This position also gives her the most clitoral friction enabling her chances of orgasm to increase.

Another aid to being pain free is to try a position that puts as little pressure as possible on the areas of your body that are painful from the cancer treatment. You can support and limit the movement of any part of your body with pillows. Supporting the shoulder and mastectomy area with pillows can limit motion. This can keep the area still and decrease any pain from movement.

With any type of perineal (muscles of the genitals) surgery, hip movements can be painful. You might choose to ask your partner to take over the hip motions if movement is painful and guide him to the speed and depth of thrusting that is comfortable for you.

Sometimes sex causes anxiety due to anticipating pain. Some options are listening to a relaxation tape before lovemaking or asking your husband to give you a total body massage to relax you before sex.

Women need to show and tell their partners what areas of their bodies are tender and which types of touches are comfortable, as well as what type of touches are painful. Women often think their husbands can read their minds and don't realize that the husband can be as anxious as or even more anxious than she is. Showing her husband what she needs can decrease the woman's anxiety as well as the man's.

Shirley came to see me complaining that she felt major rejection from her husband, Ed, after her hysterectomy for cancer. She related that he'd never talked to her about the cancer or the surgery. He hadn't even tried to initiate sex, even though her doctor had said it was okay to proceed. He had been distant and she felt he was pulling back from their relationship.

When I interviewed Ed, he was sad and confused. He was so anxious about upsetting her that he felt like he was walking on eggshells when she was around. He was afraid sex would hurt her. He also was afraid to bring up the subject of sex, cancer, or surgery because "he didn't want to remind her of it and depress her." He felt that, by keeping the status quo and going on about their lives without bothering her for sex or talking about anything unpleasant, he was protecting his wife. Sadly, what he had meant as *protection*, she had viewed as *rejection*.

The worst enemy of good sex is silence.

As you can see from their story, the worst enemy of good sex is silence. Happily, treating Shirley and Ed was a joy once they both realized they wanted the same things but had differing perceptions of what was going on. They had some difficulty with pain during intercourse, but by following some of the previous suggestions, they were back on track with their sexuality in a matter of weeks.

It's a good idea to develop a nonverbal signal that means, "Stop, that's hurting," since shouting "ouch" is a major turnoff and usually results in the end of the lovemaking. This can be part of the plan of action for how you will deal with anticipated side effects. As with other medical challenges, plan your lovemaking around the time your medication peaks.

Lack of Desire and the Grieving Process

Lack of desire can be caused by many things. I discussed the importance of having your testosterone levels checked in an earlier chapter on hormones, but it's worth mentioning again. Testosterone gel can be applied to the vulva or thigh and Joy Gel™

(compounded Viagra®, Arginine, and Isosorbide) can be applied to the clitoris. This can increase sensation and desire.

Normal grieving about the loss of health, or loss of a body part, or feeling as if you are getting old is common after cancer surgery. The stages of grief are denial, depression, anger, bargaining or the "if only" stage, and finally acceptance. It takes anywhere from one to two years to really grieve a major loss and these stages are not consecutive—they are random. You can even feel all five stages in one day or even one hour. Knowing that it's normal to careen through these emotions after loss can help you feel less crazy. We grieve equal to our loss, so if your loss is great, your grief will be as well. Minimizing grief or denying it only delays working through it and getting on with life. Remember, hasty grief is denial.

However, the depression of grief can deepen into clinical depression and may require medication. If there are any signs of suicidal thoughts or plans, sadness and constant crying every day, changes in eating or sleeping habits, feelings of hopelessness or helplessness—please see a doctor or psychiatrist and be evaluated for clinical depression and the need for antidepressant medication.

It's imperative to take time to grieve. Also realize that your partner will be grieving, so be aware of his feelings as well. Talking out feelings, praying out feelings, or writing out feelings are the best ways to traverse grief. Psalm 147:3 says, "He [God] heals the brokenhearted and binds up their wounds." God grieves with us and never leaves us or forsakes us.

Body Image before and after Cancer

Negative thinking can affect us sexually. It isn't what happens in life that is as crucial as what we *tell ourselves* about what happens to us. If you aren't feeling sexual and everything else checks out, there may be some "stinking thinking" going on. It's vital to refute negative messages with positive truth. Memorizing Scriptures that debate your negative thinking is a good way to stop the thoughts. Just disproving the harmful thoughts with positive ones is helpful as well.

Instead of telling yourself, *I'm so scarred and ugly, who would want to have sex with me?* You can answer yourself with, *I'm someone with intelligence, a sense of humor, and I love to have a good time.*

What we tell ourselves has a lot to do with our feelings and our actions. Thoughts precede feelings and feelings precede behavior. That is why surrounding yourself with positive thoughts, Scripture, and positive people will help you recover at a faster rate.

Body image problems are pervasive, even when a woman does not have cancer. So much so that there is an actual term for the unhappiness you feel about how you think your body looks—normative discontent. This means that the majority of women from puberty on up have been taught by society and our culture to be discontent with their bodies, no matter what they look like. And this discontent is so pervasive it's being called normal.

So it's no wonder that almost any woman who undergoes cancer treatment struggles with body image issues. Most people don't feel like the perfect ten, but after cancer treatment, body image and self-esteem can fall to a three or four. Whether it's loss of hair or bodily scarring, a woman may have enough discomfort with her looks that it interferes with her sex life since a woman needs to feel pretty or sexy to her mate. Sadly, too often sexual attractiveness is judged only according to the skin-deep kind of beauty, not the inner beauty a woman possesses.

Women tend to compare themselves to other women and always think they are less than the other woman. After cancer it's very easy to focus only on the affected part of the body. You feel certain that everyone is looking right at that part. It's easy to "awfulize" and imagine things worse than they are. It's hard to put things in perspective when you're so focused on your injured part. In Galatians 5:26 we are told, "Do not be self-absorbed, provoking and envying each other." Each of us is God's original. It's better to be a first-class *you* than a second-class somebody else. Comparing yourself with others only leads to two negative things—pride about yourself or inferiority about yourself. Love and accept yourself the way that God loves you, but don't be so consumed with yourself that you only value and identify with others in correlation to how they make you feel about yourself.

A woman can help improve her body image by disguising the changes made by cancer and drawing attention to her best features. I often instruct a client to get all dressed up and stand in front of a full-length mirror. She is then to look at herself from head to toe, saying only positive things about each area of her body as she goes. I have her practice this over and over until every time she looks in the mirror her mind skips past the old negative comments and goes naturally to the positive ones she has rehearsed.

Then I have the client do the same exercise dressed in a nice negligee. Next, I have her practice this in the nude, again stating only the positive things about each body part. Finally, when the woman is ready, I encourage her to do this exercise naked with her husband and let him say something positive about every aspect of his wife's body.

This exercise can take months, and rushing it is not helpful. When done carefully and sincerely, by the end of the exercise, the woman can usually think of three positive things about her body before she even thinks of one negative. And some of the positive things her husband says will be emblazoned on her mind.

Body image problems cause a woman to focus on her physical self to the exclusion of other aspects of her identity. We have a social self, a spiritual self, and an achieving self. It's good to look at all the other "selves" and see the positive aspects of each one.

Your *social self* involves all the people who love you, not for what you look like, but for who you are inside. Think of your family, friends, church friends, workpeople, and neighbors that are concerned about and care about you. Let yourself imagine their love, energy, and affirmation flowing into you, empowering you with their positive feelings about you.

Then focus on your *spiritual self.* Call upon your faith in Jesus Christ and what God says about you in the Bible.

He says you are precious and one of a kind, you are his little lamb, and the apple of his eye (1 Pet. 2:4; Isa. 40:11; Ps. 17:8).

He chose you before the creation of the world; you are so valuable to him that he paid for you with the precious blood of his Son (Eph. 1:4; 1 Pet. 1:18, 19).

He says he is as near as your next breath and that you are top priority to him, not a last-minute detail (Ps. 139:1–10; Matt. 10:31).

He promised that he will cause *all* things to work for your good (Rom. 8:28).

He won't give you any more than you can bear, but will always be available to help you carry the load (1 Cor. 10:13; Matt. 11:29, 30).

Meditating on these truths can help dispel negative feelings about your spiritual self.

Finally, the *achieving self* is that part of you that has put in maximum effort and achievement all your life. We tend to overlook or minimize our own achievements. Sometimes it's helpful to ask a beloved friend or family member to help you remember all you've achieved in life. Look at the whole picture of your life, instead of just focusing on how you have failed. We certainly should give God the glory for our abilities and accomplishments, but remembering our successes and feeling good about them is not the same thing as pride. God instructs us to have an accurate view of ourselves—our strengths and our weaknesses—so that we can serve him honestly and faithfully (Rom. 12:3–8).

Cancer changes your body—but you as a person can become stronger, happier, and more beautiful than ever. With education, patience, prayer, kindness, and love, you and your husband can actually become closer—including in the bedroom.

Points to Consider

1. Communicate with your doctor and ask him when you can resume sex, what limitations you need to observe with sex, and any side effects you need to be aware of from your cancer treatment.
2. Communicate with your husband regarding a plan of action to handle any side effects your doctor has described. Forewarned is forearmed. Look into new attitudes, new touches, and new positions.
3. Keep a positive attitude. Practice makes perfect—keep practicing staying positive in the face of any challenges.
4. Make sex a priority. After cancer, spontaneity may go out the window. Planning sex around your energy, your pain tolerance, and your desire is essential.

5. Expect the unexpected and have a sense of humor. Laugh if the Astroglide squirts on the wall or the lubricant makes you slip around like two greased sea lions. Taking sex too seriously takes all the fun out of it and only increases anxiety.
6. Consider sex therapy. It is a brief therapy that focuses on a specific sexual problem. The goal of this therapy is anxiety reduction, sexual education, and sexual enhancement. Find a counselor who is board certified in Human Sexuality. Ask for references of previous clients who are willing to waive confidentiality to talk to a new client.

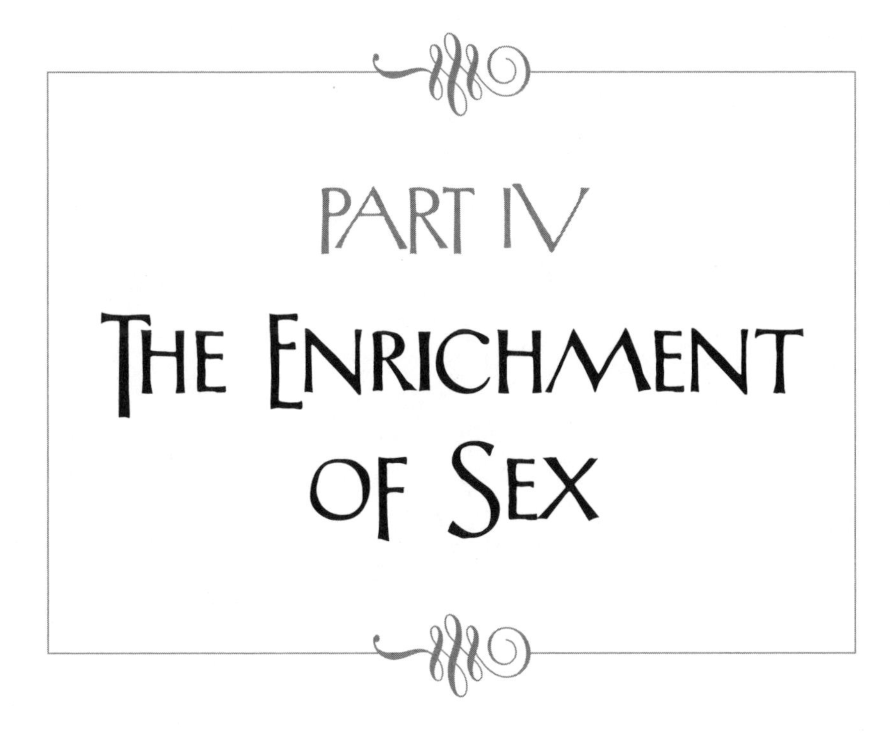

PART IV
The Enrichment of Sex

Creative Sexual Communication

The real art of conversation is not only to say the right thing in the right place but to leave unsaid the wrong thing at the tempting moment.

Lady Dorothy Nevill

Let's look in on Mr. and Mrs. Smith:

Husband: Hey, honey, would you like to have sex tonight?

Wife: Why do you *always* wait until it's so late and I'm exhausted? You're so selfish. All you care about is you. Anyway, I told you earlier I didn't want to have sex.

Husband: I thought you just meant you weren't in the mood then. I was being considerate by waiting until now, but I should have known you'd be ignoring me like you always do.

Wife: Considerate? You don't even know what the word means. You don't care about my feelings; you just want to get your needs met. You are just like your father.

Husband: Well it's been four days. Not that you'd notice. You're so wrapped up in everyone else but me, just like your mother.

Wife: Oh, that's right, bash my mother and play the martyr. Poor baby—always gets ignored.

Husband: That's right. All my friends have sex much more often than we do because you're so frigid.

Wife: I'll give you frigid. You can go sleep on the couch and you'll feel my chill all the way in the living room.

Husband: That's fine with me. I wouldn't have sex with you if you were the last woman on earth.

Ephesians 4:25–27 says, "Therefore each of you must put off falsehood and speak truthfully . . . 'In your anger do not sin': Do not let the sun go down while you are still angry, and do not give the devil a foothold."

In light of this Scripture, Mr. and Mrs. Smith both missed the mark by a mile. They spoke in anger, called each other names, dragged in other family members, went to bed angry, and were anything but patient, kind, and slow to anger. She needed consideration and he needed understanding.

Keeping this Scripture in mind, let's look in on how a different couple, Mr. and Mrs. Jones, might address the same issue.

Husband: Hey honey, what can I do to help you so we might be able to fit in a little loving tonight?

Wife: Boy, I'd really like to, but it's getting late and I have things to do that you can't help me with. I wish you would have suggested this earlier.

Husband: Watching that beautiful body of yours just made it occur to me or I would have.

Wife: You are one sweet talker, but it doesn't change the fact that I'm really tired tonight.

Husband: I know you've been working extra hard lately and maybe I could help you by giving you a total body massage. No expectations on my part, I promise. If it turns into something more, we'll go for it; if you still aren't up for it, we'll plan on tomorrow night. Deal?

Wife: Okay—if you're still awake when I finish my work. But I get a whole body massage before I decide on any sexual stuff, okay?

Husband: You got it!

This couple's communication began with Mr. Jones acknowledging that his wife was working hard that evening. Mrs. Jones affirmed her husband when she said that she would like to have sex (so that he knew she wasn't rejecting him), but she was honest about the things she had left to do.

Mr. Jones expressed consideration to his wife by answering her with a loving comment about her attractiveness, instead of getting angry that she wasn't doing exactly what he wanted. When she expressed her fatigue, he came up with a good compromise. He'd give her a massage with no expectations, and she could decide from there where it would lead. She still chose to finish her work, but she was ready to compromise by planning on the massage and possibly something more.

Why It's Difficult to Talk about Sex

It's difficult to communicate about everyday issues in a marriage, let alone *sex*. Women who grew up in homes where sexual words were never spoken may be embarrassed. Not knowing the words to use is complicated by the cultural idea that women should be passive and men should know everything there ever was to know about sex. Other women may be afraid of rejection, abandonment, or anger if their husband does not like what they have to say.

But healthy communication is crucial to developing and sustaining intimacy. One woman told me she thought lovemaking wouldn't be spontaneous if she ever discussed sexuality with her husband.

We know that most couples have had problems in sex for a long time before we ever see them. Women and men suffer in silence about this topic and tolerate frustrating or unhappy situations without seeking help. However, with education, patience, and prayer almost all sexual difficulties can be resolved or at least improved upon.

What Is Good Sexual Communication?

The definition of communication is "to convey information about; to make known." But that is only one part of the equation. Communication is information that comes from the heart and head of one person and is heard and understood by the heart and head of the other person. It has been said that communication is 7 percent the actual words we say, 38 percent tone of voice, and 55 percent facial expression and body language.[1] In sex, more than any other type of communication, body language says volumes. A marriage that does not take time to communicate with words, voice tone, and touch is a marriage headed over a cliff.

A marriage that does not take time to communicate with words, voice tone, and touch is a marriage headed over a cliff.

Satisfying sex is so much more than just two orgasms. It involves *communication* (relating verbally with a kind tone of voice and positive body language), then *closeness* (emotional and nonsexual affection), followed by *arousal* (affectionate foreplay), and then *intercourse.*

Most couples are hesitant to talk about sex at all. Many have tried but have been unsuccessful because of three typical communication offenses.

First, *being too vague about the message* or not being specific enough so that the other person understands the difficulty. An example of this message is: "You know, we should probably think about our sex troubles."

Second, *sending mixed messages.* These are messages that say two contradictory things at once. A mixed message sounds like this: "Sex was really great last night; too bad I didn't have an orgasm."

Third, *not saying what you really mean to say.* For example, you say, "You must have been really tired after we had sex last night." But what you really mean is, "You were asleep in thirty seconds and I'm disappointed because you had said we could cuddle before you went to sleep."

Many times a husband or wife in counseling will say, "Why didn't you ever tell me that before today?" I hope this chapter will stimulate your sexual communication so that you don't have to hear or say those words.

Prerequisites to Communication

Before you begin an honest sexual discussion, you must lay a good relational foundation. Certain prerequisites allow a discussion to go more smoothly and yield better results.

First, *establish trust.* Women in particular have a strong need to be assured that they can trust their husbands. Both the husband and wife must know that the other will keep any sexual conversations confidential.

Second, *pray about what you want to say.* Ask God to open your heart to communicate lovingly and to soften your husband's heart to hear you.

Third, *be sensitive to timing.* Before you communicate, choose a time when you aren't tired, or upset in any way. Most books discourage bringing up sexual problems after sex, but some couples prefer the instant replay. Just make sure it's a time when you feel as if you are both emotionally connecting. But don't put it off or procrastinate, either. Waiting too long can deepen your anger and resentment. Ephesians 4:26 says, "Don't let the sun go down while you are still angry."

I encourage my clients to begin addressing a conflict within the first twenty-four hours, if at all possible. Old anger, like battery acid, turns into bitterness and can have a smoldering effect on our minds and our bodies.

Communicating Wisely

Now that you've set the stage, learning how to communicate can make or break a talk. If you need to, follow these recommendations exactly as you would a prescription from your physician.

1. ***Begin with praise.***

Start the conversation by using "you" statements that praise and edify. Romans 14:19 tells us that we must, "make every effort to do what leads to peace and to mutual edification." We need to praise each other to success: "You are kind and considerate, so I know that I can share this with you."

Dr. John Gottman has studied relationships for many years. He states that in a happy marriage couples make at least five times as many positive statements as negative statements to and about each other and their relationship.[2]

Be honest and truthful, but emphasize what he does *right.* Tell your husband what he does for you sexually and that you think is terrific. Then use "I" messages to convey the feelings or thoughts that you'd like to express: "John, you are such a patient and considerate lover. You don't make me feel rushed or hurried, and I'm so thankful for that. I sometimes feel pressured to make every sexual encounter we have a grand event and, occasionally, I just would like to have sex without all the bells and whistles."

This type of communication cuts down on defensiveness in your husband and allows you to take responsibility for your own feelings and needs.

2. ***Be concise.***

Know what you want to say. Only tackle one issue at a time. Remember to communicate in short chunks. Prioritize and condense the most important thing you want to convey—preferably into one sentence. This will be easier for him to remember and will give your point more importance.

3. ***Check your body language.***

Make sure your body language is saying the same thing your mouth is saying. Sitting with your arms and legs crossed says, "My mind is made up; don't confuse me with the facts." Be sure to directly face your spouse and give him your full, undivided attention. Ask him to do the same so you have his undivided attention as well.

When I see clients in my office, I position my chair so that I'm directly facing them, eye to eye, shoulder to shoulder. I nod at appropriate times and ask pertinent questions. This body language says, "You are the most important person this hour and I am intently listening to everything you have to say."

Listen with your head, your heart, and your body. Someone said that God gave us two ears and one mouth so we could listen twice as much as we talk.

Don't interrupt or try to talk someone out of how they feel. Just really listen to the message that is being shared. When you are not listening actively you are giving your husband a busy signal.

4. ***Summarize and clarify.***

After one person shares the concern of their heart, the other spouse should paraphrase what they *think* the first one said. This feedback tells the communicator whether they said exactly what they meant to say and if the other person *heard* exactly what they meant to convey.

At times, a couple's communication can be like the old game we used to play called Whisper Down the Lane or Telephone. By the time the whispered sentence went down a row of people it came out sounding nothing like it was said originally. If your spouse doesn't paraphrase what you said, you will never know if he heard what it was you intended to transmit.

For example, John could reply, "So what I'm hearing you say, Mary, is that you enjoy the gourmet way we make love, but sometimes you would prefer it was the no-frills kind of sex."

If that is what you meant, say so. "Yes, that's exactly what I meant."

If it's not, resend the message and try to clarify your points. This type of summarizing not only clarifies the message, but also validates the person who sent it.

When your husband has effectively heard you, it's his turn to respond. When he does, don't defend, justify, or explain your position. Just listen and paraphrase what he said. Then, together, begin to brainstorm ways to resolve the issue together.

Don't think you have to agree with everything that is said to be a good communicator. Attempt to stay objective and nondefensive, while giving and receiving communication. Listening well and correctly summarizing the message does not have to mean you agree—it means you are good at listening to one another, recognizing your differences, and showing empathy for your spouse. God expects unity, not uniformity, and we can walk arm in arm without seeing eye to eye on every issue.[3]

Remember that each person's perception is their reality. We each see things through our own pair of glasses. Good communicating is like exchanging glasses.

5. ***Be gentle.***

Speak the truth lovingly, not out of anger or hate. Proverbs 15:1, says, "A gentle answer turns away wrath but a harsh word stirs up anger." Give what you want to say a good deal of thought and chose your words carefully.

Instead of saying, "I can't stand the way you do that," you might say, "Could we try doing it this way tonight?" Let your spouse know that objecting to a certain behavior in sex is not rejecting him. Make sure you separate the message from the man.

One client shared that her husband told her he hated the way she kissed him. She felt as if he was rejecting all of her and all of her sexuality, not just the kissing. Most of what we worked on in counseling was helping her forgive him for that cutting statement.

Evaluating Your Communication

One tool for communicating that we use in our clinic is the sexual communication quiz. This is helpful because, as couples gather data from their spouse, each person must stop and think about her or his *own* needs and feelings. Also, since sex is such a difficult topic for some couples to discuss, this quiz is an icebreaker that gives them an opportunity to write the answers down before we talk about them. I've included it on page 191 so that you can take this quiz with your husband and see how well you know each other sexually.

Effective Conflict Resolution

In his book titled, *Anger: Taming the Beast,* Reneau Peurifoy describes these three styles of conflict management: Nonassertive, Assertive, and Aggressive.[4]

The *Nonassertive* style of managing conflict is indirect and avoids conflict at all costs. This person may bottle up their anger or sulk and pout. Or the person may become passive-aggressive—getting back at others in indirect ways. The problem with this style, Peurifoy states, is that it results in internal conflicts and irritation and is less likely to result in any change.

When Bill wouldn't initiate sex as often as Kathy wanted, she would give him the silent treatment and refuse to admit anything

Sexual Communication Quiz

1. What does your spouse like best about having sex with you?
2. Would your spouse like more or less sex in your relationship?
3. Is your spouse satisfied with the amount of foreplay in your sexuality?
4. Is there anything your spouse would like to try sexually that you have not tried yet?
5. Is sex as exciting to your spouse as they would like it to be?
6. What first sexually attracted your partner to you?
7. What are the top three erogenous zones your spouse would name—for themselves?
8. Have you ever shared with your spouse your top three erogenous zones? What are they?
9. Are there sexual issues that you would like to talk to your spouse about, but have been afraid to do so? What are they?
10. How would you like your spouse to initiate intimacy?
11. Do you know how your spouse views manual stimulation without intercourse? Oral sex? Sexual toys? Does he or she know your views? What are they?
12. Are you aware of the sexual signs of aging that your spouse may exhibit and how to handle them?
13. Does your spouse know how your hormones and aging may change your system?
14. Are you willing to practice learning how to communicate about a topic you may feel uncomfortable discussing at first?

was wrong. Since Bill couldn't read her mind to know that she was upset, he didn't know he needed to respond to her. Kathy would fume internally and build up resentment toward him. Eventually, he'd initiate sex, and then Kathy would pay him back by not being interested. They both worked long and hard on helping Kathy communicate openly and directly about her needs, feelings, and anger.

The second style of managing conflict is the healthiest and comes closest to the biblical admonition to "speak the truth in love." In the *Assertive* style the person is direct but not hostile. The goal of this style is to express one's needs and wants and to resolve conflicts in a way that is satisfying to both the individual and the spouse. We teach that healthy couples can resolve conflict by one of these ways:

Compromise. Anthony wanted sex five times a week and his wife, Andrea, wanted sex twice a week. They settled on three times one week and four the next. Both compromised and it was a win-win situation.

Alternating giving in. This is like a compromise, but one time the wife gets to choose where and how they will have sex and the next time the husband gets to decide. However, all behaviors must be mutually acceptable to both partners.

One couple always fought about where they would go to eat for their date night. Needless to say, their date night rarely ended in the sexually satisfying experience they both wanted. It wasn't until I assigned the planning of date night to the wife the first and third weekends and the husband the second and fourth that they were able to give in. This couple had power-struggle issues and it helped them to know whose turn it was to be in control.

Agree to disagree without being disagreeable. This is a simple way to end an argument—but people never consider this an option.

Both people can hold onto their viewpoints without trying endlessly to convince the other that their opinion is wrong.

Barbara and Danny came to see me because they had been fighting over birth control and could come to no resolution. Barb was angry with Danny because he wouldn't get a vasectomy and Danny wanted Barb to get her tubes tied. After we discussed the merits of both, I introduced several other forms of birth control that they had not even considered. Though neither had changed their mind about their first preference, they were able to bury the hatchet and become close again.

The third style of conflict resolution is the *Aggressive* style. The person who uses this style has as their goal to dominate and get their own way. This typically ends up with others feeling hostile and defensive. Although the aggressor may think they have won, they have really lost. The other person may give in, but not happily.

Cheryl and Ken fought continually about frequency of sex. He would use guilt, anger, and frank begging until Cheryl would have sex with him. However, she felt resentful and used, eventually shutting down sexually and feeling very averse to sex. Once Ken admitted to his style of managing conflict, he was open to changing it.

Dr. John Gottman reports that happy couples can sometimes repair a situation before conflict gets in full swing. Successful repair attempts include using humor, stroking your husband with a caring remark ("I understand that this is hard for you"), making it clear you are on common ground ("This is our problem"), and offering signs of appreciation for your husband and his feelings along the way ("I really appreciate and want to thank you for . . ."). If an argument gets too heated, take a twenty-minute break and approach the topic when you are both calm.[5]

Rights and Responsibilities in Conflict Resolution

Reneau Peurifoy argues that healthy assertive behavior is rooted in a balanced set of beliefs about a person's rights and responsibilities. He cites a list of nine rights and responsibilities that assertive people maintain. Problems arise when a person wants to have the right, but not the responsibility (or even vice versa).

Rights and Responsibilities

1. ***I have the right to be treated with dignity and respect.***

I have the responsibility to treat others with dignity and respect.

2. ***I have the right to decide what is best for me.***

I have the responsibility to allow others to decide what is best for them.

3. ***I have the right to ask for what I want and need.***

I have the responsibility to allow others to refuse my request, even though I might not like being refused.

4. ***I have the right to have and express my feelings and opinions.***

I have the responsibility to express those feelings and opinions respectfully, in love, without insults or name calling.

5. ***I have the right to say no without feeling guilty.***

I have the responsibility to allow others to say no to me.

6. ***I have the right to be listened to and taken seriously.***

I have the responsibility to listen to others and take them seriously.

7. ***I have the right to make mistakes.***

I have the responsibility to accept the consequences of those mistakes.

8. ***I have the right to all of my weaknesses and limitations without shame.***

I have the responsibility to be compassionate toward others' weaknesses without ridiculing or resenting them.

9. ***I have the right to do what is necessary to protect my mental and physical health even though it may disappoint others.***

I have the responsibility to do this in a way that causes the least amount of discomfort for myself and others.[6]

These rights and responsibilities help communication by giving a framework for healthy, positive relationships. Couples who learn how to improve their communication style regarding their sexuality can reap great rewards in intimacy and connectedness. Love is patient, kind, and forgiving. All three of those qualities are the best foundation for good communication.

Points to Consider

1. Healthy communication is crucial to developing and sustaining intimacy.
2. Most couples are uncomfortable discussing sexuality.
3. Many couples suffer in silence before seeking help.
4. Poor communication results when people are too vague, give mixed messages, or don't say what they really mean.
5. There are five steps to healthy communication.
6. We are actively listening when we listen with our head and our heart, paraphrase back to our partner what we think we heard them say, and wait for verification before we respond with our point.
7. Healthy couples can pass the Sexual Communication Quiz.

8. There are three styles of conflict resolution, with the Assertive style being the healthiest and most positive way of resolving conflict.
9. Assertive styles of conflict resolution can compromise, alternate giving in, or agree to disagree without being disagreeable.
10. Assertive individuals believe in a list of nine rights and responsibilities that make communicating clear and fair.

CHAPTER 14

Twenty Secrets to Magnificent Monogamy

Love is not love, which alters
when it alteration finds.
William Shakespeare

"Sex just isn't exciting anymore!" complained Heather, a soft-spoken, intelligent woman whom I had seen a few times before. "My husband and I have been married for twenty-one years, and I think we're just bored with each other. It's always the same old routine. Even though I have an orgasm, I just feel like I'm missing out on something."

I feel like our sex life is a great Chinese restaurant that we've gone to thousands of times. Now I'm ready to try Thai.

Too often, the couples we see in counseling who have been married for a while think monogamy is monotony. Unlike the animals, our sexual desire is much more than a need to reproduce. Women value sex as an expression of love for and from their husband, as well as a means to access the pleasures of their own bodies.

After recognizing her libido in puberty, a woman believes that she will maintain and improve her sexual excitement for the rest of her life. Sadly, many times that does not prove to be true. Heather had made it through the stress of finding the right mate, maintaining her virginity until marriage, the major task of child-rearing, the ups and downs of PMS, the hormonal loss and hot flashes of menopause, body changes, changes in her health with age, and cultural expectations—only to find that when she had time to really enjoy her mate, sex had become mundane.

"Lately, I feel like our sex life is a great Chinese restaurant that we've gone to thousands of times. Now I'm ready to try Thai."

I discussed with Heather the causes for mundane monogamy such as lack of motivation, habit, apathy, being in a sexual rut, worrying about what your partner will think if you want to change things, not knowing exactly how to discuss changing things, and not knowing what to try. She was very receptive to putting the *zing* back into their romantic relationship. She realized it would take effort and planning; it wouldn't just materialize on its own. I suggested she go home and talk with her husband about our session.

Heather's husband, Jeff, was excited that his wife had taken the initiative to come see me. He admitted that he, too, was ready for some spice in their relationship. He did have some concerns and asked to have a session with me. When we met, he told me that he'd always had questions about doing anything except the missionary position. He had been taught that some sexual positions and practices were not biblical.

After beating around the bush, Jeff finally revealed his real question. "Isn't oral sex wrong from a Christian perspective, Dr. Shay?" He thought that oral sex was not biblical, but he didn't know why or where the Bible said it was wrong.

What about Oral Sex?

Since the Bible is silent on oral sex, many people assume it is wrong. Others believe that if it was forbidden, God would have forbidden it like he did other sexual practices—incest, prostitution, and sex between people and animals. I believe that oral sex is a biblically neutral behavior and each couple will have to decide for themselves what is best for them. If both partners are willing and want to experience this, I believe it can be a wonderful asset to adding variety to your lovemaking.

To answer Jeff's question, I showed him some passages in the Song of Songs where oral sex might be insinuated. In chapter four King Solomon is describing his bride on their wedding night. He seems to begin his exploration, first with her eyes, then her hair, her teeth, her lips, her neck, and her breasts, and then works his way down to the "mountain of myrrh and to the hill of incense."

In verse sixteen, the bride responds with "Let my lover come into his garden and taste its choice fruits."

Later in Song of Songs 5:1, the groom declares, "I have come into my garden, my promised bride, I have gathered my myrrh with my balsam and spice. I have eaten my honeycomb with my honey and have drunk my wine with your milk." Then God responds and says, "Eat, O friends, and drink your fill, O lovers."

I left Jeff to his own interpretation, and he agreed to do more research as to what the Bible says about marital sexuality. Jeff already knew that God created sex as a good gift for his children, but he also wanted to follow God's guidance for using that gift to bless his wife, never to hurt her.

When we discussed this new possibility at our session the next week, Heather responded that she felt comfortable with the idea of trying oral sex. She was excited about trying something new and different. When Heather and Jeff began to explore sexual expressions together, their mundane relationship evolved into an exciting and joyful reawakening of their intimacy.

As a wife, you may have concerns about feeling safe and protected while enjoying the freedom to explore your own sexuality with your husband. As I explained to Jeff, Ephesians 5:25 admonishes, "Husbands, love your wives as Christ loved the church, and gave himself up for her." If a man would truly die for his wife and place her desires ahead of his own, there is a slim chance that there would be deviancy from God's guidelines for sex. Even when a sexual practice is morally okay, if the woman is not comfortable with it, it is neither loving nor right for a husband to ask for it.

I believe these guidelines also will preclude any behaviors like anal sex which can hurt the female body. Anal sex can stretch the female anal sphincter resulting in stool seepage or tear the anus resulting in anal fissures or rectal tears.

> Even when a sexual practice is morally okay, if the woman is not comfortable with it, it is neither loving nor right for a husband to ask for it.

The Gifts of Ecstasy and Novelty

In *The Hunger for Ecstasy*, Jalaja Bonheim writes: "Ecstasy is our birthright and we need that state of feeling totally in love with life just as we need food and drink."[1] But after the biochemistry of infatuation does its work, ecstasy needs to be nourished like a plant. It doesn't grow automatically—we must consciously invite it in and make space for it.

Bonheim goes on to say that the word *ecstasy* comes from the Greek *ekstasis,* which means to stand outside oneself.

> Although we sometimes become bored by how mundane our lives can be, we cling to the familiar. We seek security in it. But ecstasy requires bursting out of ourselves and being willing to move beyond the comforts of routine to experience ourselves in the nakedness of each new moment. However, it does not mean abandoning limits and boundaries; it just means being open to change. This doesn't necessarily mean a huge time commitment, just an adjustment of consciousness.[2]

Another reason for incorporating changes in our sex lives is that novelty raises the levels of a brain chemical called dopamine. This hormone is associated with romantic love. Dopamine heightens the sex drive and gives one a feeling of euphoria and exhilaration, says Helen Fisher, a leading anthropologist at Rutgers University.[3] Novelty is originality, uniqueness, and innovation. The more we are able to be original and unique in our sexuality, the more we'll experience romantic love and a heightened sex drive. It never ceases to amaze me that couples will spend hours planning a vacation or work hard at staying physically fit and strong, but won't put any time into keeping their sexual relationship fresh and exciting. Novelty can drive the apathy away.

Novelty benefits both women and men.

In his book, *The Psychobiology of Mind Body Healing,* Ernest L. Rossi explains that novelty, enrichment, and exercise all create brain growth.[4] Maybe that's why so many people who live long and healthy lives are interesting, keep working at something they love, stay active, and are open to new ideas. I, for one, want my mind and brain to keep growing—not to stagnate or begin dying.

Now I'm not suggesting that every sexual experience need be a three-hour feast. Use the ideas from this chapter for those times when you have the time and energy for some novelty in your lovemaking.

Over the years I've developed a discovery book of ideas to help couples put the fun back into their sexuality. The ability to play and laugh makes or breaks a couple's intimacy. Sex should be an enjoyable, delightful event, not something you have to be so serious about. So ponder the following secrets and see if you can find one that gets your engine running.

Twenty Secrets to Magnificent Monogamy

1. *"Wait and See!"*

Delaying gratification is one of the best aphrodisiacs. Anticipation is a wonderful way to enhance later participation. Pick a weekend day when you can spend all day together. Start by having some heavy foreplay when you wake up but then stop, get dressed, have breakfast, and go shopping.

Every time you have a quasi-private moment touch each other, kiss, or give your husband a glimpse of something sensual: lift your skirt and show him the top of your thigh or reveal your cleavage by loosening your blouse. By the time you get home you should both be aroused and sex will be better than ever. Anticipation instills the thrill of the chase, and most men like to hunt. The longer the anticipation builds, the more exciting sex will be.

2. *"Eye Love You!"*

It's no secret that men are visual creatures—so flaunt your naked body by dusting the living room or reading a magazine "au naturel." Act as if you weren't aware he was coming home and let him catch you. Of course, lock all the doors and make sure no one else is home or expected home but him. We don't want you ripping out magazine pages to cover yourself if your mother-in-law drops in unexpectedly.

The groom in Song of Songs 4:7 exclaimed, "O my love how beautiful you are. There is no flaw in you!" Let your husband enjoy the fact that God made him to be stimulated visually. You may find your fire is lighted as well.

3. *"Shower Power"*

Hit the shower for hot and steamy sex. Anne Hooper, a sex therapist and author of *Great Sex Games,* says "the shower is basically a 'sexual nirvana.' It combines heat, pressure, moisture, and friction all in one device. It doesn't require batteries, is self-cleaning, and is installed in nearly every living space."[5] You can wash each other with a sexy-smelling body soap. This will thrill most women because we like our men clean. Try a pumpkin pie scent since Alan Hirsch, M.D., director of the Smell and Taste Treatment and Research Foundation and author of *Scent-sational Sex,* reports that pumpkin pie scent significantly increases blood flow to the penis.

4. *"Hotel Happiness"*

Go to a hotel. For most women, there is nothing quite like making love away from home. A nice hotel gives women the feeling that they are away from it all. Hotel sex is great for women since we don't have to wash the towels or change the bed, and we can relax a little more because we're not worrying about the cleanup.

5. *"Vibrating Toys"*

Don't be afraid to experiment with some toys. Vibrators come in every size and color and there is nothing wrong with asking your partner if you can't add a little "hum" to your lovemaking. The vibrator can be used to stimulate her clitoris or stimulate the head and shaft of his penis. It's not intended to take the place of the man, just possibly add a little novelty to your lovemaking.

Dr. Kevin Leman, in his book *Sheet Music,* says, "There is nothing in the Bible that prohibits the use of such marital enhancers, provided that nothing is degrading to, or unwanted by, either partner. As a way to provide variety within the marriage, the occasional use of toys can be a very good idea."[6]

A man who will try this is a man who really trusts his wife and has built a great deal of intimacy with her since he is not afraid to try new things. Many men might feel threatened at first, but as sexologist Susan Crain Bakos says, "If a woman wasn't satisfied with a man's performance, she'd be faking her orgasms and using the vibrator behind his back."[7]

6. *"Masseuse Each Other"*

A unique gift of touch is to give each other after-work massages. With only fifteen minutes of massage, you literally rub cortisol, a stress hormone, out of each other's systems.[8] Many women are so filled with stress and tension that they have little or no interest in sex. Once the stress is relieved, the thought of touching more private, sensitive areas becomes inviting.

Again, Song of Songs 6:2 says, "My lover has gone down to his garden to the beds of spices, to browse in the gardens and to gather lilies. I am my lover's and my lover is mine; he browses among the lilies."

Everyone could use a little more browsing.

7. *"Play Manicurist"*

Touch each other in simple ways. Offer to give him a manicure by just filing his nails, cutting his cuticles, and massaging his hands slowly. Because your hands have many more touch receptors than the rest of your body, just touching hands reconnects you to your partner. He can reciprocate with a hand massage or by brushing your hair or, if you are really brave, polishing your toenails.

8. *"Play 'Bored' Games"*

Change good old Monopoly into *strip* Monopoly. Each time you build a hotel, you get to ask your partner to take off one piece of clothing. Or play strip Parcheesi, or strip Scrabble. Let your novel side come out and make a "bored" game a new and *stimulating* adventure.

9. *"Our First Date!"*

Recreate a time when you felt close and connected. Go back to that little Italian restaurant he took you to for dinner on your first date and reminisce. Go to the boat marina where you sat in the car and made out after you walked along the beach. Repeating familiar experiences can bring back old emotions and perceptions, and you'll reexperience those old feel-good times. And before you leave, tell your husband you have no panties on. Just knowing that will put him into overdrive.

10. *"Dining In"*

Have a picnic in any room of the house except the kitchen or dining room. Spread a blanket on the floor and eat hamburgers and cokes while watching your favorite romantic movie. For dessert serve something that calls for a can of whipped cream. Practice squirting it on erogenous zones and licking it off of one another.

11. *"Baby Your Baby"*

If your husband has had a bad day, send him straight to bed. Allow him to rest after a hard day while you cook up eggs and bacon or French toast and give him breakfast in bed—with you as the dessert. End it with a cherry on top.

12. *"Words of Love"*

Find a book both of you will like and take turns reading the pages to each other while lying naked in bed. Love poems are great, and so is the Song of Songs in the Bible. Reading the Song of Songs aloud together will allow both of you to see just how romantic and exciting that book really is. Try the Amplified Version as it makes some of the poetic language clearer.

You can even read *Sports Illustrated* or *Reader's Digest,* because whoever is not doing the reading can massage or kiss the other person anywhere they want to. The goal is to finish one chapter or one story, which usually never happens. Remember, sex is about being fun! This sexual activity can end up being both hilarious and sensual.

13. *"Feed the Need"*

Decide to cook something you've never cooked before and cook it with your husband. Afterward, feed each other the dinner. The rules of this game are you are not allowed to feed yourself; you must feed each other. Make sure you give him a few bites with your fingers and let him suck or lick your fingers when you are finished. Then do the same with his fingers. This can be a wonderful turn-on. There is something sensuous about feeding your partner, and again, it can end in laughter and sexuality.

14. *"Sexy Dancing"*

Put on a golden oldies CD and dance to the music like you did when you were dating—but this time you'll be wearing sexy lingerie and he'll be in silk boxers. In the privacy of your home you can dance anyway you want to. Make sure you end with slow love songs so you can be close and sensuous.

15. *"Change Your Agenda"*

Most couples who have had years of sex have an itinerary when it comes to lovemaking. Change the routine from the same old kissing for five minutes, breast fondling for five minutes, genital touching for five minutes, and then intercourse. Talk with your mate and vary your itinerary, perhaps by using some of the prior suggestions. If you've taken the Sexual Communication Quiz in chapter thirteen, incorporate the new and different ideas from this quiz—the special strokes, touches, and positions that you discovered were pleasurable to one another.

16. *"Baby . . . Oh Baby!"*

Sound is very important to a man. I hear men complain in our therapy sessions that they don't know what their wives like because they're mute during sex. For a man, it's like shadow boxing when there is no feedback. Try moaning, sucking in your breath, or just saying "oh baby" when he does something you like. Actions like pulling him closer or digging your nails lightly into his back or buttocks also help him know when he's on the right track. This spurs a man to continue doing whatever it takes to bring you to orgasm. Trust me on this one. He'll work hard at remembering every time you gave him positive feedback.

17. *"Clothed Sex"*

Have sex with your clothes on for a change. Just try pushing everything to the side or up and down. It gives sex that forbidden feel—while being perfectly pure—and can add new zest to sex.

18. *"Camping Out"*

Try making love in the backyard in a tent with all the wonderful sounds of nature around you. Please note: the kids should be sent to the grandparents for an overnight stay if you try this. You don't want any little hands unzipping the tent.

19. *"Set the Stage"*

Make your bedroom more sexually friendly. Try buying red sheets, putting a red bulb in the lamp, and leaving Astroglide and candles accessible on the bedside table. Make sure you have a CD player in the bedroom and together buy some music you both think of as romantic or sexy.

20. *"Oral Options"*

Try licking and tasting your lover in an unexplored part of his body—and let him taste you there, too.

Knees—The underside of our knees is very sensitive.

Stomach—Dip your tongue into the belly button and explore the stomach.

Mouth—Lick along the bottom lip and give extra time to the corners of the mouth. Do the same with the top lip.

Thigh—Trace the spot from inner knee to the underwear crease and back again. Repeat with other leg.

Feet—First, make sure you've both hit the showers. Then give a good foot massage, and end by kissing each toe.
Chest—Suck a cooling mint and then encircle the nipple. End with blowing on it to give a thrilling sensation.
Hand—Encircle his palm with tiny tongue licks and end by sucking each fingertip.

I hope that at least one of these ideas will get you and your partner purring. So, what are you waiting for? Put this book down and *just do it!*

Notes

Chapter 1

1. Donna Wong, *Essentials of Pediatric Nursing* (St. Louis: Mosby Publishing, 1997), 66.

2. Helen Fisher, *The Anatomy of Love* (New York: Norton and Company, 1992), 37–51.

3. John Money, *Lovemaps* (New York: Irvington Publishers, 1993), 19.

4. Helen Fisher, *The First Sex* (New York: Random House, 1999), 231.

5. Fisher, *The Anatomy of Love,* 53.

6. Ibid., 51–58.

7. Ibid.

Chapter 2

1. David Ferguson and Chris Thurmond, *The Pursuit of Intimacy* (Nashville, Nelson Publishers, 1993), 46.

2. Ferguson and Thurmond, 43.

Chapter 3

1. Margaret Mahler, Fred Pine, and Anni Bergman, *The Psychological Birth of the Human Infant* (New York: Basic Books, 2000), Concepts from chapters 3–7.

2. Henry Cloud and John Townsend, *Boundaries* (Grand Rapids: Zondervan, 1992), 70.

3. Frank Minirth, Paul Meier, and Stephen Arterburn, *The Complete Life Encyclopedia* (Nashville: Thomas Nelson Publishers, 1995), 175.

4. Cloud and Townsend, 72–73.

5. David Ferguson and Chris Thurmond, *In Pursuit of Intimacy* (Nashville: Nelson Publishers, 1993), 68–69.

Chapter 4

1. John Eldredge, *Wild at Heart* (Nashville: Thomas Nelson Publishing, 2001), 49.

2. Robert T. Michael, et al., *Sex in America: A Definitive Survey* (New York: Little, Brown, 1994).

3. Shere Hite, *The Hite Report* (New York: Bantum Doubleday Dell, 1981).

Chapter 5

1. Leslie Schover, *Sexuality and Cancer* (New York: The American Cancer Society, 1988), 4.

2. Hilda Hutcherson, *What Your Mother Never Told You about Sex* (New York: Penguin Putnam Publishing, 2002), 23.

3. Hutcherson, 24.

4. Albert Allgeier and Elizabeth Allgeier, *Sexual Interactions* (Lexington: D.C. Heath and Co., 1995), 475.

5. Helen Singer Kaplan, *The New Sex Therapy* (New York: Random House Inc., 1974).

Chapter 6

1. William Masters, Virginia Johnson, and Robert Kolodny, *Human Sexuality* (Boston: Little, Brown, 1985), 78.

2. Albert Allgeier and Elizabeth Allgeier, *Sexual Interactions* (Lexington: D. C. Heath and Co., 1995), 219.

3. Erwin J. Berle, *The Sex Atlas* (New York: Continuum, 1983), 65.

4. Masters, Johnson, and Kolodny, 86–88.

5. Allgeier and Allgeier, 219.

Chapter 7

1. Janice DeMasters, *Everywoman: The Essential Guide for Healthy Living* (New York: Profile Pursuit Publishers, 2002), 108.

2. Edward Klaiber, *Hormones and the Mind* (New York: Harper Collins Publishers, 2001), 34–35.

3. Judith Reichman, *I'm Not in the Mood* (New York: Morrow Publishers, 1998), 64.

4. Klaiber, 51.

5. Susan Rako, *The Hormone of Desire* (New York: Three Rivers Press, 1996), 63.

6. Reichman, 29.

7. Patricia Ladewig, Marcia London, and Sally Olds, *Essentials of Maternal-Newborn Nursing* (Redwood City: Benjamin/Cummings Publishing Co., 1994), 519.

8. Ibid., 778.

9. Ibid., 808.

10. Reichman, 31.

11. Ibid.

12. DeMasters, 5.

13. "Risks and Benefits of Estrogen Plus Progestin in Healthy Postmenopausal Women: Principal Results from the Women's Health Initiative Randomized Controlled Trial," *Journal of American Medical Association,* 288:321–333.

14. Michael Smith, "Hormone Replacement Trial Halted," Web MD Medical News, October 24, 2002.

15. Schairer et al., "Estrogen-Progestin Replacement and Risk of Breast Cancer," *Journal of American Medical Association,* 284:691–694.

Chapter 8

1. Kim Folstad. "Sex? What's That?" *St. Petersberg Times,* August 12, 2003, 3D.

2. Archibald D. Hart, Catherine Hart Weber, and Debra L. Taylor, *Secrets of Eve* (Nashville: Word Publishing, 1998), 197.

Chapter 9

1. Shere Hite, *The Hite Report* (New York: Bantum Doubleday Bell, 1981).

2. Judith Reichman, *I'm Not in the Mood* (New York: William Morrow and Co., 1998), 66–72.

3. Patricia Ladewig, Marcia London, and Sally Olds, *Essentials of Maternal-Newborn Nursing* (Redwood City: Benjamin/Cummings Publishing Co., 1994), 808.

4. Reichman, 12–13.

Chapter 10

1. Hershel Chicowitz, "The Baby Boomer Headquarters," <http://www.bbhq.com/whatsabm.htm>, accessed Aug. 28, 2003.

2. Debora Demeter, “Sex and the Elderly,” <http://www.umkc.edu/sites/hsw/age>, accessed Sept. 4, 2003.

3. Patricia Bloom, “Sex after Sixty: Demystifying the Elderly Taboo,” <http://sexhealth/webcast_transcript.asp?f+sexual_health&c+healthyaging_sextabo>, accessed Sept. 4, 2003.

4. E. M. Brecher and the Editors of Consumer Reports Books, *Love, Sex, and Aging* (Boston: Little, Brown, 1984), 29.

5. Albert Allgeier and Elizabeth Allgeier, *Sexual Interaction* (Lexington: D. C. Heath and Co., 1995), 441.

6. Tiffany Fields, *Psychology Today,* March/April 2000, 41.

Chapter 11

1. <http://americanheart.org/presenter.jhtml?identifier=3053>.

2. Judith Reichman, *I'm Not in the Mood* (New York: Morrow, 1998), 74.

3. Sharon Lewis, Idolia Collier, and Margaret Heitkemper, *Medical Surgical Nursing* (St. Louis: Mosby Publishing, 1992), 1438.

4. Ibid., 1766.

5. Ibid., 1767.

6. Christopher P. Silveri, MD, “The Spine Universe,” <http://www.spineuniverse.com/displayarticle.php/article1932.html>.

Chapter 13

1. A. Mehrabian, *Nonverbal Communication* (Chicago: Aldine Atherton, 1972).

2. John Gottman and Nan Silver, *The Seven Principles for Making Marriage Work* (New York: Random House, 2001), Chapter 4.

3. Rick Warren, *The Purpose Driven Life* (Grand Rapids: Zondervan, 2002), 158.

4. Reneau Peurifoy, *Anger: Taming the Beast* (New York: Kodansha, 1999), 147–148.

5. Gottman and Silver, Chapter 6.

6. Peurifoy, 153.

Chapter 14

1. Jalaja Bonheim, *The Hunger for Ecstasy* (Emmaus, PA: Rodale, 2001), Chapter 1.

2. Ibid.

3. Helen Fisher, *The First Sex* (New York: Random House, 1999), 231.

4. Ernest Lawrence Rossi, *The Psychobiology of Mind Body Healing* (New York: W. W. Norton: 1986).

5. Anne Hooper, *Great Sex Games* (New York: Dorling Kindersley Publishing, 2000).

6. Kevin Leman, *Sheet Music: Uncovering the Secrets of Sexual Intimacy in Marriage* (Wheaton: Tyndale House Publishers, 2003), 165–166.

7. Susan Crain Bakos, *Sexual Pleasures: What Women Really Want, What Women Really Need* (New York: St. Martin's Press, 1992).

8. Gordon Inkeles, *Unwinding: Super Massage for Stress Control* (New York: Weidenfeld and Nicolson, 1988).

List of Terms

Anus is the opening to the rectum and the exit for bowel waste.

Anxiety is a perceived future-oriented threat.

Bonding needs are emotional needs that cause us to feel fulfilled and satisfied when met.

Brain chemicals that regulate mood are serotonin, norepinephrine, and dopamine.

Cervix is the neck-shaped structure at the opening to the uterus.

Cesarean section is a surgical incision through the abdominal wall and uterus performed to deliver a baby.

Clitoris is a female organ that looks like a tiny button of flesh. It has an extremely dense network of blood vessels and nerves which makes it supersensitive to touch and stimulation. The sole purpose of the clitoris is pleasure, and it is the trigger of orgasm for most females.

Commitment is a state of being emotionally, intellectually, and spiritually bound to another person.

Dependency is a problem of emotional limits or boundaries. The dependent person is so enmeshed with another that they don't know where they end and the other begins. They look to others for approval and affirmation. This state is normal in small children but should decrease as the child matures.

Desire is the thought, or the physical or emotional feeling, of being willing to participate in sex or to seek it out.

Differentiation is the second stage of individuation.

Episiotomy is a surgical incision from the vagina down into the perineum or area between the vagina and anus which allows for easier childbirth.

Estrogen is one of the most significant hormones for females and is produced by the ovaries, adrenal glands, and in the fatty tissues.

Fallopian tubes are two slender ducts where eggs pass from the ovaries to the uterus.

Fantasy is an imagined event or sequence of mental images, such as a daydream.

Female Orgasmic Disorder or FOD is a persistent or recurrent delay in, or absence of orgasm following, a normal sexual excitement phase.

FLASH is an acronym that stands for the five basic emotions: Fear, Love, Anger, Sadness, and Happiness.

Follicle Stimulating Hormone (FSH) test is a hormone test which verifies the onset of menopause or perimenopause.

G-spot is a bumpy area the size of a dime on the front wall of a woman's vagina.

Genitalia are the reproductive organs and the external sexual organs.

Hormone Replacement Therapy or HRT is one hormone or a combination of hormones given as a treatment for relief from menopausal symptoms.

Hymen is the fragile tissue that surrounds the vagina without completely covering it.

Individuation is the slow gradual act of breaking away from dependency into a person who can identify and recognize their own needs and get them met in a healthy way.

Infatuation is an extravagant attraction or passion.

Kegel exercises involve isolating and contracting the muscles that allow the squeezing of the vagina.

Libido is sexual desire.

Limbic system is the part of the brain that has as one of its functions the seat of long-term memory.

Lovemaps are mental maps or patterns developed very early in life in response to family or friends or a combination thereof. Many times we use these mental maps as patterns for the partners we choose.

Mastectomy is the removal of a woman's breast.

Menopause is the period marked by the natural and permanent cessation of menstruation, occurring typically between the ages of forty-five and fifty-five.

Olfactory nerves are the nerves that enable us to smell.

Orgasm is when the body suddenly discharges its accumulated sexual tension in a peak of sexual arousal.

Ovaries are two almond-shaped reproductive organs that produce eggs, estrogen, progesterone, and testosterone.

Parental engrossment is the behaviors that occur when the parents are engrossed and begin to bond with their infant.

PEA is short for phenylethylamine, a natural stimulant secreted during infatuation.

Perimenopause is the few years in a woman's life that precede menopause.

Perineum is the area between the vagina and the anus.

Practicing is the third stage of individuation.

Premenstrual Syndrome is a group of symptoms that occurs after ovulation when there is a change in estrogen and progesterone levels. For some women, this change brings on symptoms of tension, irritability, emotional ups and downs, bloating, breast tenderness, sadness, headaches, and food cravings. These symptoms are often called PMS.

Progesterone is a hormone that is produced in the ovaries. It protects us from too much estrogen before menopause.

Prolactin is a hormone secreted by the pituitary gland that stimulates milk production.

Pubococcygeus muscles or PC muscles are the muscles that surround the vagina.

Rapprochement is the fourth stage of individuation.

Sensate focus exercises are exercises that were designed by Masters and Johnson to help couples overcome performance anxiety and get in touch with their sensuous feelings.

Sexual Response Cycle is a cycle of four stages that humans go through while having sex. The four stages are excitement, plateau, orgasm, and resolution.

Symbiosis is a relationship of dependence and is the first stage of individuation.

Tactile is a word derived from the Latin meaning "to touch."

Testosterone is a hormone that generates desire and produces a biological sexual response. It is secreted in the ovaries and adrenal glands.

Urethra is the opening to the bladder.

Uterus is the hollow muscular reproductive organ in which the fertilized egg implants and develops.

Vagina is the passage that leads from an opening in the external sexual anatomy to the cervix or mouth of the uterus.

Vaginal prolapse is a bulging of the bladder or rectum into the vagina.

Vulva is the external genital organs of the female.

About the Author

Dr. Shay Roop, RN, LMHC, EdD, is a Florida licensed mental health counselor and is board certified in Human Sexuality by the American Board of Sexology. She is also a member of the American Board of Christian Sex Therapists and is a Florida licensed Registered Nurse.

Dr. Roop completed her undergraduate work in psychology at St. Joseph's College in Windham, Maine, and received her Master's Degree in Counseling from Nova Southeastern in Ft. Lauderdale, Florida. Her Doctoral degree is from the Institute for the Advanced Study of Human Sexuality in California.

Dr. Roop and her husband, Dr. Bob Roop, own and run Professional Counseling in Clearwater, Florida. She specializes in women's and adolescent's issues, sexual dysfunction, depression, anxiety, and relationship issues.

They have three children, Kelly, Steve, and Laura, and one son-in-love, Patrick, who is married to Kelly.

Both Shay and Bob have given marriage seminars in numerous churches. The most popular seminar title is, "Ten Tips to Make Your Marriage Sizzle." Dr. Shay is also available to speak to women's groups on relationship issues, sexual issues, or women's issues in general.

For information on how to contact Dr. Shay Roop or invite her to speak to your group, check her website, www.drshay.org, or write to her at Drshay911@aol.com.